CAPITAL PUNISHMENT

London's Places of Execution

Robert Bard

Acknowledgements

I would like to thank the following for their assistance, suggestions, and interest in the writing of this book: Sandra Steer, Paul Capell, Lynne Dearling, Sebastian Stock, Ian Southern, Gideon Kay, Simon Whitaker, Jon and Wendy Kennedy, and Simone and Martin Box.

For Bradley Oscar Stock

First published 2016

Amberley Publishing
The Hill, Stroud
Gloucestershire, GL5 4EP

www.amberley-books.com

Copyright © Robert Bard, 2016

The right of Robert Bard to be identified as the Author of this work has been asserted in accordance with the Copyrights, Designs and Patents Act 1988.

All rights reserved. No part of this book may be reprinted or reproduced or utilised in any form or by any electronic, mechanical or other means, now known or hereafter invented, including photocopying and recording, or in any information storage or retrieval system, without the permission in writing from the Publishers.

British Library Cataloguing in Publication Data.
A catalogue record for this book is available from the British Library.

ISBN 978 1 4456 6736 2 (print)
ISBN 978 1 4456 6737 9 (ebook)

Origination by Amberley Publishing.
Printed in Great Britain.

Contents

	Introduction	4
1.	Execution and London Society: Some Grim Realities	8
2.	Tyburn	16
3.	St Giles-in-the Fields	28
4.	Newgate	31
5.	Charing Cross	39
6.	Old and New Palace Yards, Westminster	44
7.	Tower Green	53
8.	Tower Hill	61
9.	Lincoln's Inn Fields	74
10.	St Paul's Churchyard	77
11.	Smithfield	81
12.	Wapping	83
13.	Kennington Common	87
14.	Some Other London Places of Execution	90
	Bibliography	94

Introduction

London and Its Executions

Executions have always held a morbid fascination for the population of London. Aside from the arguments for and against capital punishment, even now the almost clinical methods of execution employed by the United States still excite ghoulish media attention.

London played host to a number of sites of execution, some well known such as the Tower of London and Tyburn, some less well known such as Smithfield, Charing Cross, Kennington Common, Bunhill Fields, Bethnal Green, and Clerkenwell Green. The *Newgate Calendar* even tells us that a Patrick McCarty was executed at the bottom of Bow Street, Covent Garden, Westminster, on 24 October 1760, for murder. London, thus, was a city, the like of which we could only imagine, in the way in

A mother points out to her child the consequences of crime: the gibbet.

which Londoners were confronted with death, and the instruments of death and punishment at every turn. Charles Dickens wrote on the subject as to whether capital punishment acted as a deterrent. To determine this he questioned whether those who attended executions were put off of crime,

> There never is (and there never was) an execution at the Old Bailey in London, but the spectators include two large classes of thieves – one class who go there as they would go to a dog-fight, or any other brutal sport, for the attraction and excitement of the spectacle; the other who make it a dry matter of business, and mix with the crowd solely to pick pockets. Add to these, the dissolute, the drunken, the most idle, profligate, and abandoned of both sexes – some moody ill-conditioned minds, drawn thither by a fearful interest – and some impelled by curiosity; of whom the greater part are of an age and temperament rendering the gratification of that curiosity highly dangerous to themselves and to society...

For Dickens, executions were no more than entertainment for the London mob who turned out in large numbers for these executions. The mob varied in size, with possibly up to 100,000 attending a single execution, but more typically numbering between 3,000 and 40,000. Executions took place at Tyburn and Newgate eight times a year.

Rituals and expectations associated with execution developed over the centuries. It was seen as important for the victim to undergo a 'good death', which meant showing bravado, indifference to one's fate and an acceptable, entertaining final speech. These were often transcribed and sold to the waiting mob, frequently before even having been spoken. However, the majority of felons were so scared that they couldn't even speak during the course of their last public performance. Some of these unfortunates were popular with the crowd and excited pity and shouts of support in their final moments, others roused jeers and were pelted.

The *Newgate Calendar*, a generic name for a series of volumes that detailed the lives and deaths of many eighteenth-century criminals was one of those books, along with the Bible, *Foxe's book of Martyrs* and *The Pilgrim's Progress*, most likely to be found in any middle-class English home between 1750 and 1850. It was compiled by the Deputy Keeper of Newgate, who would write on a long parchment the names of all those admitted to the gaol during the previous month. Children were encouraged to read it because it was believed to inculcate principles of right living by fear of punishment, if not by the dull and earnest morals appended to the stories of highwaymen and other felons. The editors of one version even included as a frontispiece a picture of a devoted mother (*see illustration on page 4*) giving a copy to her young son, while pointing out the window at a body hanging on a gibbet.

The *Newgate Calendar*, or *Malefactors' Bloody Register*, was originally published in five volumes in 1760, dealing with crimes from 1700 to 1760. It appeared in many further editions from 1820 as the *Newgate Calendar*. Between 1863 and 1865 it was published weekly as the *New Newgate Calendar*. There was an almost obsessive preoccupation with London's criminals and their fate, justified within the wrapper of morals and learning. Accounts of executions and the dying words of the condemned were printed and sold as popular literature in the form of broadsheets or chapbooks (cheap books). As will be seen when looking at the individual sites of execution and their associated rituals, the condemned were subjected to a tortuous drawn-out final journey, the best documented of which was that from Newgate Gaol to the gallows barely 3 miles away at Tyburn. It was customary for the procession of carts, usually two or three with the prisoners and a chaplain, to stop en route from Newgate to Tyburn at the St Sepulchre Church opposite Newgate. Here, friends would present the condemned with bouquets that would be stuck on their breast buttonholes, acting as a nosegay. This tradition continued until 1774. The procession would then move on and stop in Holborn, St Giles in the Fields near the site of Centre Point, Tottenham Court Road, for the condemned to have a last cup of ale. There are many contemporary comments that often the prisoners were launched into eternity 'in a state of wild intoxication'. Inevitably, a mixture of alcohol and bravado led to frequent interchanges between the crowd and the condemned. The *London Magazine* of July 1735 tells us that at an execution on Monday 21, 'five of the condemned malefactors were executed at Tyburn' We are told that the occupants of the second of two carts 'behaved very audaciously, calling out to the populace, and laughing aloud several times', though the magazine optimistically comments that alcohol could not have played a part as it was banned by the Lord Mayor and Aldermen.

Some of London's most prominent citizens have left accounts of attending executions. One such person, Samuel Pepys, observed the hanging of a Colonel James Turner, whom he happened to know, and failed to see the irony when he seemed more concerned with his own discomfort than that of his former acquaintance while attempting to watch his demise. He wrote in his diary,

> 21 January 1664
> Up; and after sending my wife to my aunt Wight's to get a place to see Turner hanged, I to the office, where we sat all the morning. And at noon, going to the Change and seeing people flock in that, I enquired and found that Turner was not yet hanged; and so I went among them to Leadenhall Street at the end of Lyme Street, near where the robbery was done, and so to St Mary Axe, where he lived; and there I got for a shilling to stand upon the wheel of a cart, in great pain, above an hour before the execution was done...

It is apparent that for Pepys attending Turner's execution was nothing more than a convenient diversion and a not unpleasant way to while away a couple of hours.

Undoubtedly one of the attractions of attending an execution was based on an attempt to judge the behaviour of the condemned against the belief of how one would behave under similar circumstances. It is important to remember that in twenty-first-century Britain, we have generally become far more humane, with a belief that human life is valuable and to be preserved at most cost. Death in the Middle Ages has been described as a craft. Twenty-first-century life in the western world has sanitised death. Today it can be controlled, delayed, and often timed. Our forefathers lived with it in every form. The plague and influenza cut swathes through the population of Elizabethan England.

The imagery of death comes to prominence in the funerary art of sixteenth-century England. In life there is death. Death was communal: 'the deathbed was likely to be a busy and noisy place, even if for once the dying got to occupy the bed alone; it was open not merely to the immediate family but to other solidarities of which the dying person was a member.' On his deathbed Charles II actually apologised to those attending him, saying that 'he had been a most unconscionable time dying; but hoped they would excuse it.' Further, we are told that even at this time (the sixteenth and seventeenth centuries) a 'good death' was important.

The debate concerning the rights and wrongs of execution as a punishment did not arise until persons such as Lord Palmerston, Charles Dickens and William Makepeace Thackeray called for abolition in the 1840s. When I started to research the victims, and visit the sites, I believed that many of the victims of judicial death, in particular the Lords Kilmarnock and Balmerino, and Lord William Russell were extremely brave, and principled persons – they handled their own mortality immaculately. It was not until I became almost totally immersed in the writings of the sixteenth, seventeenth, and eighteenth centuries that I realised what the writer Leslie Poles Hartley meant by his observation that 'the past is a foreign country; they do things differently there.' Early so-called civilised England is a country of the past that we can barely comprehend. The rules were different; the people were different; society that regarded itself as superior and cultured in reality lacked the veneer that we call civilisation, and this lack of veneer allowed basic, untamed, and savage instincts to impregnate society at all levels. Even children were at risk of paying the ultimate price for their misdemeanours. Life really was cheap. It was only after 1800 that child hangings became unusual, and warranted comment. The last child to be hanged in England was fourteen-year-old John Bell, for killing another boy and robbing the corpse. He was executed at Rochester in Kent, 1831.

The language of the time gives a flavour of the contemporary thinking that attended these executions. I have also selected accounts that allow us some insight into the persons or people concerned, and used eyewitness reports that penetrate the veneer of scaffold bravery. I have also used reports from contemporaries that reflect some of-the time notions on the whole business of public execution. Where available I have used old illustrations alongside my own modern photographs in order to allow a modern-day perspective against that of an earlier time.

1. Execution and London Society: Some Grim Realities

Death at the hands of the state has been the subject of much academic study. The rituals associated with execution have received increasingly detailed attention. It is postulated that the condemned man's dying speech, which usually admitted the crime and blessed the monarch, was an admission of the legitimacy of the power of the state by which they would die.

Between the 1680s and the 1720s the number of offences punishable by death rose from around eighty to over 350. The pro-rata number of executions did not, however, increase in direct proportion because the number of deaths was mitigated by transportation to the colonies, and in some cases pardons. The death penalty was meant to act as a warning. It is clear from the volumes of literature about crime and society from the sixteenth to the nineteenth centuries that, for many, the possibility of dying on the gallows was merely an occupational hazard. For some it was a chance to play a central, pivotal role for a morning and, through bravado and repartee with the assembled mob, be remembered in the ballads and chapbooks by future generations. Indeed, many who would have died in total obscurity still survive to us by virtue of the *Newgate Calendar*.

Royalty and aristocracy could expect to meet death at the hands of the headsman. This headsman was optimistically expected to offer eternity with a single blow of the axe, either within the Tower of London or Tower Green, so that the privileged few could die in relative privacy. Tower Hill was where many aristocrats and members of the gentry were dispatched. The lower orders could typically expect the full penalty of the law at Tyburn or Newgate, dying by suffocation at the end of the hangman's noose. Burial was not guaranteed as many were, by sentence of law, handed over to the surgeons for anatomising. Burial, where allowed, was often under or in the vicinity of the gallows at Tyburn, or under paving stones in Newgate Gaol. Nineteenth-century building works in the vicinity of Oxford Street and Edgware Road bear testimony to this. The severity of the form of death one met depended on one's position in society. Aristocrats sentenced to be hanged, drawn and quartered, one of the most prolonged and barbaric forms of death, requested of the monarch that their sentences be 'commuted' to the comparatively humane headsman's axe. The word 'comparatively' is used because often the events on the headsman's scaffold bordered on total incompetence and butchery. Margaret Pole, Countess of Salisbury, was, in 1541 at the age of approximately seventy, executed within the walls of the Tower, and reputedly chased around the scaffold while the executioner hacked at her, taking eleven blows to dispatch her. Another execution on Tower Hill was that of James, Duke of Monmouth in 1685. The rebellious, illegitimate son of the late Charles II pleaded with his uncle, James II, for his life, but as a contender for the throne he was shown no mercy. The executioner lost his nerve and struck five times, pleaded with the mob by offering a large sum of money to anyone who would finish the job, and then continued, completing the task to the jeering of the surrounding mob by using a knife. It was customary for the aristocratic victim to pay his executioner a sum of money for the execution to be carried out cleanly. It was common for the victim to ask to see and feel the axe to ensure that it was sharp enough for the task. Charles I interrupted his final speech on two occasions to tell those on the scaffold who wanted to touch the axe to leave it alone.

After looking in detail at some of the characters who died on the scaffold or the gallows, it is clear that, in many cases, attitudes to death were very different to our own. The numerous final speeches allow an analysis of the victim's belief that they either died for a principle, or knew that they would sit in God's presence for the sacrifice they made. There is rarely any doubt expressed by the victim that he or she is going to a better place. This is common in the sixteenth and seventeenth centuries, where last-minute offers of repentance would have allowed the victim to escape the flames, and were always turned down. This indicates a powerful, unbending certainty in what lay beyond the flames.

The Reality of Execution

Man has always been particularly inventive in the methods used to despatch his fellow beings. One of the cruellest forms of punishment was that of being hanged, drawn and quartered. This was usually reserved for those convicted of treason and, probably for reasons of modesty, applied to men only. Women convicted of treason were usually burnt at the stake. Introduced by Edward I, there are records of it having been used in 1241 against a William Maurice, and again in 1283. One of the best-known victims of this method of execution was William Wallace (1270– 22 August 1305), made famous to the modern public by his somewhat inaccurate method of dispatch in the 1995 film. Some of the most notable victims of this form of execution who will be looked at in more detail are: Guy Fawkes, for his attempt to destroy the Houses of Parliament and kill James I, in 1606; and the regicides, including rather unusually three who had died a number of years earlier – Oliver Cromwell, Henry Ireton and John Bradshaw – all of whom were exhumed, and punished at Tyburn posthumously. The sentence was still in use, but considerably toned down, as late as 1820, when Arthur Thistlewood and his five accomplices were sentenced as follows:

> That you, each of you, be taken hence to the gaol from whence you came, and from thence that you be drawn on a hurdle to a place of execution, and be there hanged by the neck until dead; and that afterwards your heads shall be severed from your bodies, and your bodies divided into four quarters, to be disposed of as his Majesty shall think fit. And may God of His infinite goodness have mercy upon your souls.

The crime had been the planning, at a house in Cato Street, London, of the murder of the Prime Minister, Lord Liverpool and his cabinet. The 'drawing and quartering' was omitted from the actual execution, as was the 'drawn on a hurdle' but the victims were hanged and their heads severed after death. The house where the planning of the assassination of the government and where the conspirators were arrested can still be seen at No. 6 Cato Street in the vicinity of Edgware Road.

The reality of judicial death varied according to the means of death, the efficiency of the executioner, and the period of time in which the felon was executed. Anne Boleyn, in 1536, executed by a swordsman who 'smote off her head at one stroke', was relatively fortunate when compared to some of the victims of Jack Ketch, the executioner responsible for the beheading of Lord William Russell in 1683 and the Duke of Monmouth in 1685. He was notorious for taking several blows of the axe to remove the heads of both unfortunates. Ketch even issued an apology by way of a pamphlet in which he blamed the victims, one not having 'dispose[d] himself as was most suitable' and claimed that he was interrupted while taking aim. There was even some doubt, and still is, as to whether an efficient headsman brought about instantaneous death. The ritual of holding up the victim's head and displaying it to the crowd was designed to show the possibly still-aware felon to on lookers around the scaffold and let him or her know that they had been executed. There has been some argument that the decapitated head, which often still showed intelligent movement of the lips and eyes, was still 'alive' for anything up to twenty seconds after decapitation. English law knew no bounds to its cruelty. There are records of victims being boiled alive at Smithfield, or bungled burnings where the female victim, who should have been strangled prior to being burned, was left to die an excruciatingly loud and vocal death because the fire had been set too early and the executioner was driven back by the

No. 6 Cato Street, London, W2, where the conspirators were discovered.

flames. The victims of one of the most barbaric forms of execution – hanging, drawn and quartered – were often alive, conscious, and aware well into the proceedings. Such was the cruelty of this form of death that the hangman would ensure that the victim was cut down off the gallows before he fell into unconsciousness, so that he could appreciate the every nuance of watching his own stomach cut open before his own eyes, and see his intestines thrown into a brazier. This form of execution, within law, lasted into the nineteenth century. The form of death, however, that accounted over the centuries for most of London's victims was that of death by hanging on one of its many gallows.

Hanging as a Means of Execution

Death by hanging as a term comes nowhere near to the appalling reality as experienced by the felon. Carefully calculated drops designed to bring a clinical instantaneous death by breaking the victim's neck was a product of the 1880s and beyond. Even then the victim's heart would continue to beat for several minutes. Prior to this, death by hanging was an even slower, more painful method of asphyxiation, which could typically last up to thirty minutes, and with bungled executions, much longer. Up to an hour has been recorded. Instant death could be achieved by jumping off the scaffold ladder, where this was available, but the victim's attempt to die quickly and thereby cheat the crowd often failed. At Tyburn, typically the victim would be mounted on a horse-drawn cart that would pass under the gallows. It would then stop and a rope was put round the victim's neck (if it was not already placed round his or her neck at the start of the procession) and the cart would trundle off, leaving the victim dangling and slowly suffocating. One of the Cato Street conspirators hanged at Newgate told the hangman, 'now, old gentleman, finish me tidily: pull the rope tighter; it may slip,' then struggled on the end of the rope for five minutes.

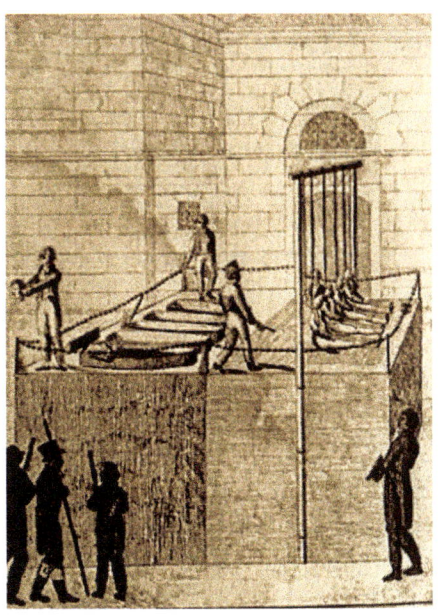

From the *Newgate Calendar*, the interior of the prison. Execution of the Cato Street conspirators, Newgate Prison, London, 1 May 1820. Some struggled slowly and painfully.

Returning to Life

Hanging as a means of death was not always reliable. It was not unusual for the families of the victims at Tyburn to wait by the gallows, undertake an unseemly fight with the waiting surgeon's assistants looking for instructional material, and after reclaiming the body, rush it off to a nearby house in order to apply various manners of resuscitation. Many a felon not due to be anatomised would request that his family or friends undertake such a task. A report from the *Daily Gazetteer* on 7 September 1736 stated,

> Bristol, Sept. 4. At 12 o'clock yesterday noon, Vernham and Harding were carried from Newgate to the place of Execution on St Michael's-Hill, attended by the Under-Sheriff and his Officers, and the Constables of the City (in a cart, with haltars [*sic*] about their necks) the Divine who attended them having finished his last office, the cart drew away; but to the surprize of every person, after being both cut down from the gallows, Vernham was perceived to have life in him when put in the coffin, and some Lightermen and others, who promised to save his body from the Surgeons, carried him away to a house near the Ferry on St Philip's Backs, and a Surgeon being sent for immediately, open'd a vein, which so recover'd his senses, that he had the use of speech, sate upright, rubbed his knees, shook hands with divers persons that he knew, and to all seeming appearance a perfect recovery was expected.

Vernham died that evening, but his associate also hanged on the same gallows; Harding also survived execution. Harding recovered and was pardoned. Frighteningly, particularly for those rapidly interred next to the gallows, this occasionally had the desired effect, leading one to wonder how many executed felons suffered the further indignity of believing they had survived the gallows, were placed in their coffins, and subsequently found they had been buried alive? Even worse are the reports of those unfortunates sentenced to be anatomised after death.

An event with a happy ending is that of the execution and subsequent recovery of Anne Greene in Oxford on 14 December 1650. She had been sentenced to die at the Oxford Assizes for the crime of infanticide. She had arranged, as was customary, for friends to hang onto her feet and strike her chest while being hanged in order to ensure a quick death. The hangman, fearing that the rope might break, asked the participants to cease their activities. After hanging for around thirty minutes, her body was taken down and placed in a coffin. The coffin was taken to the home of Dr William Petty, a lecturer in anatomy to be anatomised. The coffin was opened, with Petty and his students present, and there was not a little surprise when the 'corpse' took a breath. The intended dissection became resuscitation. We are told that the treatment for the deceased's post-death recovery was the placing of the body in an upright position, pouring hot drinks into the mouth, tickling the neck, and the rubbing of the hands and feet, followed, for good measure, by bloodletting. She was able to talk within twelve hours and was fully recovered after two days. She gained a pardon, married, and lived for a further fifteen years. There are also reports of a far more alarming nature. The *Newgate Calendar* reports the case of a surgeon working on an eighteenth-century executed German criminal who, when the felon showed signs of life, announced that he had been 'hanged for so cruel a murder, should we restore him to life, he would probably kill somebody else. I say, gentlemen, all these things considered, it is my opinion that we had better proceed in the dissection'. And this they did.

How did it feel to be hanged?

On 5 December 1705 a convicted housebreaker, John Smith, survived execution at Tyburn. The *Calendar* informs us that he was carried to Tyburn,

> Where he performed his devotions, and he was turned off in the usual manner; but when he was hung near fifteen minutes the people present cried out 'A reprieve!' Hereupon the malefactor was cut down, and being conveyed to a house in the neighbourhood, he soon recovered, in consequence of bleeding, and other proper applications.

It was inevitable that those present would ask the question as to what it was like to be hanged. Smith responded saying that,

> When he was turned off, he, for some time, was sensible of very great pain, occasioned by the weight of his body, and felt his spirits in a strange commotion, violently pressing upwards: that having forced their way to his head, he, as it were, saw a great blaze or glaring light, which seemed to go out at his eyes with a flash, and then he lost all sense of pain. That after he was cut down, and began to come to himself, the blood and spirits forcing themselves into their former channels, put him, by a sort of pricking or shooting, to such intolerable pain, that he could have wished those hanged who had cut him down.

Attending an Execution

Attendance at executions was a popular London pastime. It could be dangerous in its own right. There are many reports of scaffolds, spectator seating, or other misfortunes leading to the death of observers. A newspaper report from *The Post Man* in June 1698 graphically relates an incident that took place almost opposite Newgate, outside St Sepulchre's Church:

> Yesterday 6 of the condemned criminals were executed at Tyburn, viz. Audley who killed the apothecaries wife, Price for forging Exchequer Notes, and Brown for burglary, these 3 went in a cart. Doctor Morgan and his brother for coyning, and one Cook for coyning; these 3 went in a sledge. Just as the cart with the criminals reached the corner of St Pulchers Churchyard, a great part of the wall (on which leaned a great many spectators) fell down to the ground, by which I hear one man was killed outright, and a great many others wounded, (some say 40) some of which mortally, and it is said 4 are since dead of their wounds. This accident put a stop to the cart, so that it could not pass the usual way, but was obliged to return towards Newgate, and so go through Pye Corner, into Smithfield, and down Hosier-lane into Holbourn. The barbers apprentice for ravishing a girl is reprieved.

Boswell (1740–95), the Scottish diarist, could not resist attending an execution although the experience troubled him. At this time he was suffering from 'melancholy'; it seems a rather unusual form of spiritual uplifting to visit Newgate to observe the prisoners, then travel to Tyburn on the following day to watch the prisoners he had seen the day before be executed. On 3 May 1763, Boswell had decided on an impulse to visit Newgate Prison to 'see prisoners of one kind or other...' At Tyburn the next day, in the cells awaiting execution, were Paul Lewis, convicted of robbery, and Hannah Diego, convicted for theft. He watched them walk past him into Newgate Chapel, commenting 'the woman was a big unconcerned being...' and 'Paul ... was a genteel, spirited young fellow ... an acquaintance asked him how he was. He said, 'Very well'; quite resigned. Poor fellow! I really took a great concern for him, and wished to relieve him. He walked firmly and with a good air, with his chains rattling upon him, to the chapel.' The entry from his *London Journal* for the next day, Wednesday 4 May 1763, reads,

> My curiosity to see the melancholy spectacle of the executions was so strong that I could not resist it, although I was sensible that I would suffer much from it. In my younger years I had read in the *Lives of the Convicts* so much about Tyburn that I had a sort of horrid eagerness to be there. I also wished to see the last behaviour of Paul Lewis, the handsome fellow whom I had seen the day before. Accordingly I took Captain Temple with me, and he and I got upon a scaffold very near the fatal tree, so that we could clearly see all the dismal scene. There was a prodigious crowd of spectators. I was almost terribly shocked, and thrown into a very deep melancholy.

Thackeray, another campaigner for the abolition of the death penalty, attended a hanging that continued to haunt him: 'I can see Mr Ketch [the hangman] at this moment, with an easy air, taking the rope from his pocket ... I feel ashamed and degraded at the brutal curiosity which took me to that brutal sight; and ... I pray Almighty God to cause this disgraceful sin to pass from among us, and to cleanse our land of blood.'

One of the better known descriptions of a hanging comes from a letter by Charles Dickens that was published in the *Daily News*, where he was the editor. It relates to the hanging in July 1840 of a then-famous murderer, Courvoisier:

> I was, purposely, in the spot, from midnight of the night before; and was a near witness of the whole process of the building of the scaffold, the gathering of the crowd, the gradual swelling of the concourse with the coming-on of day, the hanging of the man, the cutting of the body down, and the removal of it into the prison. From the moment of my arrival, when there were but a few score boys in the street, and all those young thieves, and all clustered together behind the barrier nearest to the drop-down to the time when I saw the body with its dangling head, being carried on a wooden bier into the gaol-I did not see one token in all the immense crowd; at the windows, in the streets, on the house-tops, anywhere; of any one emotion suitable to the occasion. No sorrow, no salutary terror, no abhorrence, no seriousness; nothing but ribaldry, debauchery, levity, drunkenness, and flaunting vice in fifty other shapes. I should have deemed it impossible that I could have ever felt any large assemblage of

my fellow-creatures to be so odious. I hoped, for an instant, that there was some sense of Death and Eternity in the cry of 'Hats off!' when the miserable wretch appeared; but I found, next moment, that they only raised it as they would at a Play-to see the stage the better, in the final scene.

Of the effect upon a perfectly different class, I can speak with no less confidence. There were, with me, some gentlemen of education and distinction in imaginative pursuits, who had, as I had, a particular detestation of that murderer; not only for the cruel deed he had done, but for his slow and subtle treachery, and for his wicked defence. And yet, if any among us could have saved the man (we said so, afterwards, with one accord), he would have done it. It was so loathsome, pitiful, and vile a sight, that the law appeared to be as bad as he, or worse; being very much the stronger, and shedding around it a far more dismal contagion.

Reforms

The numbers of those executed in England can only be estimated, but between 1530 and 1630 probably around 75,000 people were executed, though this was a peak, the like of which never happened again. The late seventeenth century saw increasing numbers being transported to the colonies, providing an alternative to having to execute those convicted of capital crimes. Apart from a blip during the late eighteenth century, the numbers consistently reduced and continued to do so into the nineteenth century when, in 1837, a large number of the laws allowing the death penalty as a sentence were scrapped. Increasingly educated voices were being raised against the barbarity of the public ceremony, which took place in the name of the state and extinguished the lives, often slowly and painfully, of its citizens. Sir Samuel Romilly, a solicitor-general and nineteenth-century law reformer attempted to ameliorate the English criminal law, believing it to be cruel and illogical. The large number of offences punishable by death, whether the accused went to the gallows, a transport ship, or served a prison term, was totally arbitrary. Although the majority of trivial offences were commuted, the prisoner would suffer the trauma of having to hear the death sentence read out against him or her. Romilly recognised the injustice of such a system and, in 1808, he managed to repeal an Elizabethan statute that made it a capital offence to steal from the person.

There existed a contradiction within a society in which an intelligent, fun-loving and cultured monarch, Charles II, could enjoy the spectacle of the disembowelling and slow tortuous death of the regicides at Charing Cross. Colonel Harrison, one of the regicides, was 'dragged on a hurdle past Whitehall [where Charles I was executed] to Charing Cross where the statue of Charles I on horseback stands today. In the presence of a great concourse of persons, including the King himself and many ladies of the Court, he was hanged, cut down whilst still sensible, his intestines drawn out and thrown on the furnace, and his quivering body quartered.' Years later the king would listen quietly to the account of an execution he could have prevented, that of Lord William Russell in 1683. He was also happy to countenance the exhumation of Oliver Cromwell, John Bradshaw, and Henry Ireton from their respective graves in Westminster Abbey, and have them hanged and dismembered at Tyburn.

In 1832, the Punishment of Death Act reduced the number of crimes punishable by hanging by two-thirds. By 1861 the number of punishable offences had been reduced to four: murder, arson in royal dockyards, treason, and certain forms of piracy. William Ewart Gladstone, a future prime minister, and a Member of Parliament, attempted to have the death penalty abolished in 1840.

2. Tyburn

Tyburn is Britain's best known place of execution. In its near thousand years of existence, it has been estimated that the number of unfortunates who met their death there probably numbered in excess of 50,000 souls. At hangings as late as 1783 at the junction of Edgware Road, Bayswater Road and today's Oxford Street, this entire area was densely packed with rowdy mobs, pickpockets, pie sellers, and sellers of pre-printed last speeches. The crowds would have been immense, with stands set up to allow viewing for the better off. The balconies along the route from Newgate and in the immediate vicinity of the western end of Oxford Street would have been crowded with the 'better sorts' waiting for the entertainment to begin.

Early History

It is highly likely that Tyburn's origins as a place of execution was post-Norman Conquest. William I (reigned 1066–87) actually abolished capital punishment, but substituted the death penalty with tortures and mutilations that left felons without eyes or limbs. It is likely that the gallows at Tyburn were instituted under Henry I, who reigned from 1100 to 1135. Marks, in his work *Tyburn Tree*, believes that 'the institution of the gallows of Tyburn probably dates from this time. The origin of Tyburn is certainly Norman; its early name, 'The Elms,' testifies to this, for among the Normans the elm was the tree of justice.' He comments that this is the reason that 'The Elms' is similarly used in early references to Smithfield.

The first reference to Tyburn as a place of execution is in the year 1108 and a probable execution at Tyburn is given in the year 1177. The first confirmed execution appears in 1196 with William Fitz Osbert, or Osborn, who was possibly an early solicitor as he is described as being 'skilled in law'. It is highly likely that the execution was simply the first that is recorded and that executions had taken place in this vicinity for a longer period.

Another early victim of Tyburn was Sir William de Marisco, or Marsh, who was implicated in an attempt to kill the king, by cutting his throat at Woodstock in Oxfordshire. Marsh fled to his island retreat of Lundy in the Bristol Channel, from where he engaged in piracy. He was eventually captured due to the treachery of his fellow band

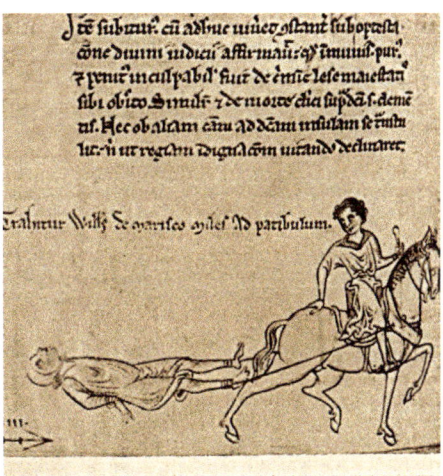

William de Marisco (William Marsh) drawn to the gallows in 1242.

of thugs. He and sixteen others were handed over to the king. For a man of violence and living in times well acquainted with death, he seems to have taken his impending demise badly. He claimed he was totally blameless in respect of the plot on the king's life, and his flight to Lundy was simply to appease the king by his absence. The plundering was accounted as a simple need to survive. Just prior to his execution it was said:

> he poured out his soul to God ... with contrition and tears he admitted his sins, not seeking to extenuate them, but even accusing himself. Therefore the friar preacher, a discreet man, who received his confession, gave him gentle consolation, and dismissed him in peace, exhorting him to suffer his punishment with patience, as a means of penance.

Then, of the punishment itself,

> First ... he was drawn from Westminster to the Tower of London, and thence to that instrument of punishment, commonly called a gibbet: when he had there breathed out his wretched soul, he was hanged on one of the hooks, and when the body was stiff it was let down and disembowelled, and the bowels were at once burnt on the spot. Then the miserable body was divided into four parts, which were sent to four of the chief cities, so that this lamentable spectacle might inspire fear in all beholders.

Location of the Tyburn Gallows

The exact location of what was London's most renowned place of execution is a matter of some debate. The site of the gallows varied over the centuries. It is however reasonably certain that they did not stand where Marble Arch is located today. Marks tells us that,

> the first information of the site of the gallows other than the vague indication of 'Tyburn' is found in one of the old chronicles, which tells that, in 1330, Mortimer was executed at 'The Elms, about a league outside the city.' The distance thus vaguely

stated would apply about equally to any one of the conjectured sites from Marylebone Lane to the head of the Serpentine, at which writers have severally placed the gallows.

Camden's *Britannica* (1607) contained a map that places the gallows, depicted as a triangular structure, situated at the north-east end of Hyde Park with the word 'Tyborne'. This is in itself evidence of the now permanent nature of the gallows. The 'triple tree', a far more industrial approach to hanging, was installed to cope with an Elizabethan crime wave in 1571. Marks believed that a controversial incident concerning the Catholic wife of Charles I acted as a method of pinpointing the location:

> On June 26th of this year, (1626) Henrietta Maria, [the French Catholic wife of Charles I] after a day spent in devotion, went with her attendants through St. James's Park to Hyde Park. Whether by accident or design she went towards Tyburn. Charles hated the Queen's French suite [courtiers], secured to her by treaty ... The courtiers made the most of the visit to Tyburn; it was averred that the Queen's confessor had made her walk barefoot to the gallows, thereby to honour the saint of the day in visiting that holy place, where so many martyrs had shed their blood in the Catholic cause.

Following the political controversy that followed, a Marshall de Bassompiere defended the queen and, by his comments, possibly fixed the site of the gallows:

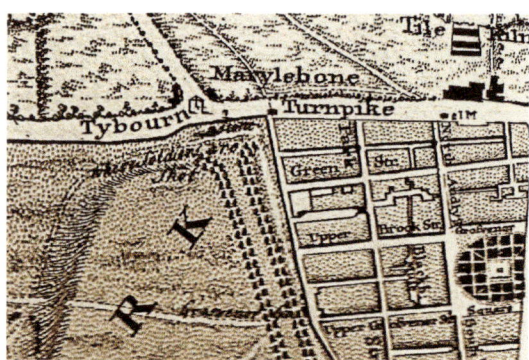

From the John Rocque map of London, 1746. In the region where Speaker's Corner is now situated is an area marked 'Where Soldiers are Shot'.

The area under the Odeon was the likely site of the burial pit where the felons were interred after execution.

Inset: View of the Tyburn Turnpike in 1813. The turnpike was situated at what is now the junction of Oxford Street and Bayswater Road.

'I know of a surety,' he said, 'that you do not believe that which you publish to others.' He declared that the Queen had not been within fifty paces of the gallows. He repeats the description of the place as at the entrance of a high road ... The words 'the entrance of a high road' fix definitely the spot indicated, approximately, by Norden's Map.

Marks believes that the road or highway referred to can be none other than Edgware Road.

John Rocque's map of 1746 (see illustration on the previous page) places the gallows near the junction of the Bayswater Road and Edgware Road. By 1759, locating the position of the gallows becomes less certain. A portable gallows were introduced which was 'put up on the day of execution and afterwards taken down'. The evidence for the removal of the Triple Tree comes from the *Whitehall Evening Post* of 4 October 1759, which says

> Yesterday morning, about Half an Hour after Nine o'clock the four malefactors were carried in two carts from Newgate, and executed on the new Moving Gallows at Tyburn ... The Gallows, after the Bodies were cut down, was carried off in a cart.

The location of the gallows is a debate eagerly picked up by *Old and New London*, published in 1878, 105 years after executions had ceased at Tyburn and been transferred to Newgate. The last execution took place in 1783.

> The exact spot on which the fatal Tyburn Tree was erected has been often discussed by antiquaries. It would appear, however, to be identified with the site of the house in the south-east corner of Connaught Square, formerly numbered 49; for in the lease granted by the Bishop of London, to whom the property belongs, this fact is particularly mentioned.

The writer then quotes from *The Antiquary* of October 1873. The article indicates that the debate as to where the gallows stood was a matter of interest and curiosity during the late nineteenth century:

> I was born within 100 yards of the exact spot on which the gallows stood, and my uncle took up the stones on which the uprights were placed. The following is his statement to me, and the circumstance of his telling it: – In 1810, when Connaught Place was being built, he was employed on the works, and for many years lived at the corner of Bryanston Street and the Edgware Road, nearly opposite Connaught Mews. My father, a master carpenter, worked for several years in Connaught Place, and on one occasion he employed his brother, I think in the year 1834; at all events, we had just left No. 6, the residence of Sir Charles Coote. It was at this time I said to my uncle, 'Now you are here, tell me where the gallows stood'; to which he replied, 'Opposite here, where the staves are.' I thereupon crossed over, and drove a brass-headed nail into the exact spot he indicated. On reaching home, I told my mother of the occurrence, and asked if it were correct. She said it was so, for she remembered the posts standing when she was a child. This might be about the year 1800; and, as she was born in Bryanston Street,

I believe she stated what she knew to be a fact. I well remember Connaught Square being built, and I also recollect a low house standing at the corner of the Uxbridge Road, close to No. 1, Connaught Place [Arklow House], and that, on the removal of this house, quantities of human bones were found. I saw them carted away by Mr. Nicholls, contractor, of Adams' Mews. He removed Tyburn toll-house in 1829. From what I have been told by old inhabitants that were born in the neighbourhood, probably about 1750, I have every reason to believe that the space from the toll-house to Frederick Mews was used as a place of execution, and the bodies buried adjacent, for I have seen the remains disinterred when the square and adjoining streets were being built.

The article continues by referring to another London history as a means of pinpointing where executions took place:

The gallows itself subsequently consisted of two uprights and a cross-beam, erected on the morning of execution across the Edgware Road, opposite the house at the corner of Upper Bryanston Street and the Edgware Road, wherein the gallows was deposited after being used; this house had curious iron balconies to the windows of the first and second floors, where the sheriffs sat to witness the executions. After the place of execution was changed to Newgate, in 1783, the gallows was bought by a carpenter, and made into stands for beer-butts in the cellars of the 'Carpenters Arms' public-house, hard by.

The Carpenters Arms Public House is still there and is located at No. 12 Seymour Place.

Thomas Smith, in his work *A Topographical and Historical Account of the Parish of St. Marylebone* (1833), tells us that the movable gallows were usually erected near the corner of Edgware Road and Bryanston Street, but the place of erection was not always exactly the same. Evidence of the differing locations of the portable gallows comes from the *Gentleman's Magazine* of 29 August 1783, which says that 'the gallows were fixed about 50 yards nearer the Park wall than usual.' As to the location of the Tyburn Turnpike, Marks tells us that

When the turnpike was in its turn removed, its position was recorded by a monument placed on the south side of the road, somewhat to the west of the Marble Arch. It is

William Hogarth, *Industry and Idleness*, Plate II: 'The Idle Prentice Executed at Tyburn', 30 September 1747.

a slab of cast iron, with a gable top, bearing on both sides the words, 'Here Stood Tyburn Gate 1829', that being the date of the abolition of the turnpike. This monument correctly indicated the position of the gate, which stretched across the road: it was not intended to show the position of the gallows, which, however, it did indicate approximately. It was necessarily removed in the improvements carried out near the Marble Arch in the spring of 1908.

This stone can still be seen, with some difficulty, behind a mortgage poster in the window of Lloyds Bank at No. 195 Edgware Road.

Some Tyburn Victims

On 23 August 1305, William Wallace was executed. While it is commonly believed that he met his death at Smithfield (where there is a plaque to his memory), it is possible, even probable, that the sentence was carried out at Tyburn:

> drawn from Westminster to the Tower and thence to Tyburn ... 'the man of Belial,' as he is constantly called in the Chronicles. Wallace was hanged on a very high gallows, especially made for the occasion ... The place of execution of Wallace was undoubtedly Tyburn. The court sentence bore that Wallace's head should be exposed on London Bridge. This is the first recorded instance of a head being exposed here.

The following year, the Earl of Athol was accused of rebellion against the king and died here on 7 November, to the delight of the ailing Edward I. Athol claimed to be of royal descent and was therefore, as a gesture from Edward, 'hanged higher than other parricides'. Royal blood had privileges – one being that he was allowed to ride on horseback to Tyburn. After being suspended, according to the chronicler, Matthew of Westminster, he was let down, half alive, 'so that his torment might be greater, very cruelly beheaded, then the body was thrown into a fire previously kindled in the sight of the sufferer, and reduced to ashes. Then the head was placed on London Bridge but higher than the rest, in regard to his royal descent'.

Another prominent execution, which took place at Tyburn on 1 July 1681, was that of Oliver Plunkett, Archbishop of Armagh. Plunkett had been convicted of high treason for promoting Catholicism and was sentenced to be hanged, drawn and quartered. One of the more remarkable consequences of this execution was that the various parts of his body travelled further after his death than they had ever done while he was alive. His remains were buried in two boxes in the churchyard of the nearby St Giles in the Fields. Two years later they were exhumed and parts sent to a Benedictine monastery near Hildesheim in Germany, while his head was sent in turn to Rome, Armagh, and finally, in 1921, Drogheda. Though some body parts stayed in Germany, others were sent to Downside Abbey, where they remain today. Plunkett was canonised in 1975.

One of the most unusual Tyburn executions was that of Earl Ferrers (b. 1720), who was executed in 1760 for the murder of his steward. Ferrers suffered from a short temper and 'lost it' with one of his servants, whom he ordered to kneel down and then, drawing a pistol, mortally wounded the man with a shot to the head. He was

The Triple Tree, *c.* 1680. The method of this execution was by slow strangulation when the cart drove on. The coffin(s) are visible in the cart behind.

held in the Tower for two months, then in April 1760 was tried before the House of Lords. He was found guilty and sentenced to be hanged on Monday 21 April, followed by being anatomised. The execution of this sentence was set for Monday 5 May. His execution caused widespread comment and excitement since it was unusual for members of the nobility to die on the gallows.

State Trials and Proceedings relates that when it was time for Ferrers to leave for the sentence to be carried out, he sent a message to the sheriffs

> requesting their permission that he might go in his own landau, which was waiting for him in the Tower, instead of the mourning-coach which had been provided by his friends; which request being granted, his lordship, attended by the reverend Mr. Humphries, the chaplain of the Tower, entered into his landau, drawn by six horses, and was conducted in it, by the officers of the Tower, to the outward gate, and there delivered into the custody of the sheriffs, upon their giving the following receipt...

The 'receipt' requested for the still-living Ferrers, was literally just that. It reads,

> Tower-Hill, 5th May, 1760:
> Received then of Charles Rainsford, esq. deputy-lieutenant of the Tower of London, the body of the within-named Laurence earl Ferrers, viscount Tamworth, delivered to us in obedience of the king's writ, of which the within is a true copy – Geo. Errington, Paul Vaillant, Sheriffs of London and Sheriff of Middlesex.

The then extensive procession comprising 'a very large body of the constables for the county of Middlesex' got under way. The slowness of the procession brought forth comment from his lordship 'that the apparatus of death, and the passing through such crowds of people, were ten times worse than death itself'. When the procession reached 'that part of Holborn which is near Drury-lane, he [Ferrers] said he was thirsty, and should be glad of a glass of wine and water; but upon the sheriff's remonstrating to him, that a stop for that purpose would necessarily draw a greater crowd about him'.

Ferrers acquiesced despite the lack of any future opportunity to enjoy a glass of wine and the procession continued. In an impressive display of calm and fortitude as the procession approached Tyburn, Ferrers asked if the procession might stop awhile while he took leave of a friend he had spotted in the crowd. The sheriff replied that 'if his lordship insisted upon it, it should be so; but that he wished his lordship, for his own sake, would decline it, lest the sight of a person, for whom he had such a regard, should unman him, and disarm him of the fortitude he possessed – to which his lordship, without the least hesitation, replied, "Sir, if you think I am wrong, I submit"' Ferrer's bravery continued when the earl's landau reached Tyburn:

> The landau being now advanced to the place of execution, his lordship alighted from it, and ascended upon the scaffold, which was covered with black baize, with the same composure and fortitude of mind he had enjoyed from the time he left the Tower; where, after a short stay, Mr Humphries asked his lordship, if he chose to say prayers? Which he declined; but upon asking him, if he did not choose to join with him in the Lord's Prayer? He readily answered, He would, for he always thought it a very fine prayer; upon which they knelt down together upon two cushions, covered with black baize, and his lordship with an audible voice very devoutly repeated the Lord's Prayer, and afterwards, with great energy, the following ejaculations, 'O God, forgive me all my errors, pardon all my sins'. His lordship then rising, took his leave of the sheriffs and the chaplain; and after thanking them for their many civilities, he presented his watch to Mr Sheriff Vaillant, which he desired his acceptance of; and signified his desire, that his body be buried at Breden or Stanton, in Leicestershire.

The moment had now come for Ferrers to depart this world, but he made a mistake when he summoned the executioner to grant his forgiveness, and paid him five guineas. In the confusion he pressed the money into the hands of the executioner's assistant. An unseemly squabble between the executioner and his assistant then broke out, which the sheriff put an end to. The final act now began:

> The executioner then proceeded to do his duty, to which his lordship, with great resignation submitted – his neckcloth being taken off, a white cap, which his lordship had brought in his pocket, being put upon his head, his arms secured by a black sash from incommoding himself, and the cord put round his neck, he advanced by three steps upon an elevation in the middle of the scaffold, where part of the floor had been raised about eighteen inches higher than the rest; and standing under the cross-beam which went over it, covered with black baize, he asked the executioner, 'Am I right?' – Then the cap upon a signal given by the sheriff was drawn over his face and then, upon a signal given by the sheriff (for his lordship, upon being before asked, declined to give one himself) that part upon which he stood, instantly sunk down from beneath his feet, and left him entirely suspended; but not having sunk down so low as was designed, it was immediately pressed down, and levelled with the rest of the floor. For a few seconds his lordship made some struggles against the attacks of death, but was soon eased of all pain by the pressure of the executioner.

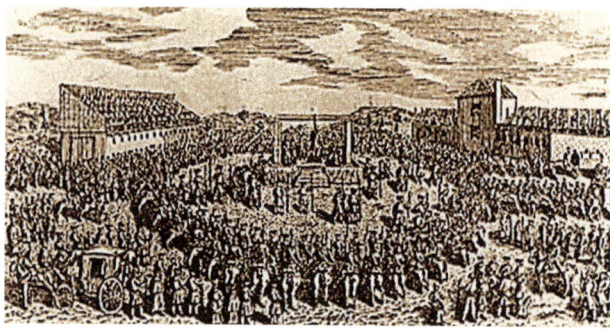

View of the execution of Earl Ferrers at Tyburn, 1760. The earl was executed for the murder of his steward.

The *State Trials and Proceedings* commented that whatever Ferrers' crime, by his behaviour during the final moments, he had earned tremendous respect and honour.

The body was left to hang for the customary period of one hour before 'the coffin was raised up, with the greater decency to receive the body, and being deposited in the hearse, was conveyed by the sheriffs with the same procession to Surgeon's Hall, near the Old Bailey to undergo the remainder of the sentence'. Where the *State Trials and Proceedings* leave off, the *Newgate Calendar* takes over and with great delight informs the reader that 'a large incision was made across the throat; the lower part of the belly was laid open, and the bowels taken away. It was afterwards publicly exposed to view in a room up one pair of stairs at the Hall; and on the evening of Thursday, the 8 of May, it was delivered to his friends for internment.'

The body was then handed over to his friends for burial; this took place at St Pancras in a grave dug to the depth, we are told, of '12 or 14 feet deep, under the belfry.' In 1782, the body was exhumed and returned to the family vault at Staunton Harold in Leicestershire.

Military Executions

In the area that is now Speaker's Corner in Hyde Park a place was set aside for military executions and other punishments. The following two entries indicate the nature of the crimes for which soldiers were punished:

15 January 1726
Wednesday last three private Centinels of the Foot-Guards were whipt in Hyde-Park; one for desertion, another for being a Papist, and the third for cursing his Colonel; the last ran the gauntlet, and the others were ty'd to a tree.
                        Weekly Journal, or *The British Gazetteer*

26 March 1726
Last Thursday John Ellis a private Centinel in Colonel Ingoldsby's Company, in the First Regiment of Foot Guards, was shot to death in Hyde-Park for desertion. About seven in the morning he was convey'd from the Savoy to the Tilt-Yard, and ten men from each Company of the three Regiments being drawn up on the parade before ten; the drums beat the Grenadiers March, when the prisoner hand-cuff'd,

and a clergyman with him, march'd on foot to the place of execution, when he seemingly died very penitent.

Weekly Journal, or *The British Gazetteer*

Burial of Tyburn Felons

What happened to the remains of executed felons? Marks devotes a whole chapter to this matter. Some probably found their way to a burial ground at Charterhouse. John Stow, writing in 1598, mentions that Ralph Stratford, Bishop of London, purchased a piece of ground at Clerkenwell in 1348 which he enclosed with a brick wall:

> He there erected a small chapel, where masses were said for the repose of the dead, and named the place Pardon Churchyard. The plague still raging, Sir Walter de Manny, that brave knight whose deeds are so proudly and prominently blazoned in the pages of Froissart, purchased of the brethren of St. Bartholomew Spital a piece of ground contiguous to Pardon Churchyard, called the Spital Croft, which the good Bishop Stratford also consecrated. The two burial-grounds, afterwards united, were known as New Church Hawe.

This Pardon churchyard took executed felons and suicides – the latter were frequently given no burial in consecrated land and were interred at crossroads. There were two Pardon churchyards – one at Charterhouse and one mentioned by Stow near St Paul's Cathedral. *The Greyfriars' Chronicle* has an entry referring to the execution and burial there of twelve Lincolnshire men and reads as follows,

> 1537. Also this yere the XXV. day of March the Lyncolnechere men that was with bishoppe Makerell was browte owte of Newgate un to the yelde-halle in roppys, and there had their jugment to be draune, hongyd, and heddyd and qwarterd, and soo was the XXIX. of March after, the wych was on Maundy thursdaye, and all their qwarters with their heddes was burryd at Pardone church yerde in the frary.

At the Reformation, the priory of St John's was suppressed, as was its cart used to transport the deceased felons.

Death brought no guarantee of burial as we have seen in those cases where bodies went to anatomy instructors. A case without a specified date, but from the sixteenth century, was that of Awfield who was refused burial. His crime had been to distribute 'lewd and traitorous books'. His local parishioners refused a traitor to be buried 'where theire parents, wyeffs, children, kynred, maisters, and old neighbours did rest: and his carcase was retourned to the buryall grounde neere Tyborne'

It is highly likely that those not sentenced to be hanged drawn and quartered, then anatomised, or those that had friends to take their bodies away, were simply flung into pits in the immediate vicinity of the gallows. In the early nineteenth century when a house was demolished in the vicinity of the fixed gallows by Connaught Place and Uxbridge Road, an eye witness says he remembers 'quantities of human bones being found.' Further, as previously noted in the section on the location of the gallows, we are told by way of an 'old inhabitant' born around 1750 that 'I have every reason to believe that the space from the toll-house [on the junction of the Edgware Road and Oxford Street] to Frederick Mews was used as a place of execution, and the bodies buried adjacent, for I have seen the remains disinterred when the square and adjoining streets were being built.' A letter to *The Times* in 9 May 1860, from a gentleman who lived in Connaught Place at the south-west corner of the Edgware Road, indicates that a burial pit for felons lay at the corner of Edgware Road and Oxford Street (*see* image below).

We know that the bones of three of the Charles I regicides lie in the vicinity of the south-west corner of Edgware Road, approximately where the Odeon Cinema Marble Arch is located. Samuel Pepys, in his diary, Tuesday 4 December 1660 comments,

> This day the Parliament voted that the bodies of Oliver, Ireton, Bradshaw, &c., should be taken up out of their graves in the Abbey, and drawn to the gallows, and there hanged and buried under it: which (methinks) do trouble me that a man of so great courage as he was, should have that dishonour, though otherwise he might deserve it enough.

The three, including Cromwell, were accordingly hanged and cut to pieces at Tyburn. Their heads were set up on poles outside Westminster Hall, but the remnants of their

A letter to *The Times* from 9 May 1860.

The statue of Oliver Cromwell in front of Westminster Hall. After the restoration of Charles II to the throne in 1661, Cromwell's body was removed from Westminster Abbey and his head placed on a pole on top of Westminster Hall.

bodies were thrown into a pit at the foot of the gallows. The original site of Cromwell's burial in Westminster Abbey can still be seen and is marked 'The Burial Place of Oliver Cromwell 1658–1661.'

The Demise of Tyburn

The continued gentrification and development of the area surrounding Tyburn and the opening of sufficient space in front of Newgate brought executions at Tyburn to a close in 1783.

Tyburn Today

Little remains of the site of Tyburn but on the last Sunday of each April a walk takes place from the Old Bailey, on the site of the Newgate Gaol, to the Tyburn Convent in Bayswater.

The Convent is at No. 8 Hyde Park Place in the Bayswater Road, approximately 300 paces east of the presumed site of the gallows.

At Tyburn Way in the middle of the Marble Arch roundabout is a reminder of the gallows, which reads,

> For 600 years this crossroads was known as Tyburn. A plaque in the traffic island at the junction of Edgware Road and Bayswater Road marks the site where gallows were thought to have stood from 1571 to 1759. The gallows were known as the Tyburn Tree but were replaced by movable gallows when a toll-house was built on the site for the turnpike road. In the eighteenth century Oxford Street was called Tyburn Road and Park Lane was Tyburn Lane. By around 1780 Oxford Street was fully built up as a residential area and the last public execution at Tyburn was held in 1783...

The plaque that marks the approximate location of the fixed gallows lies in a dangerous location on a traffic island between Bayswater Road and Edgware Road, on the left. This more or less accords with the location depicted in the Rocque map of London from 1746.

Plaque on the wall of the Tyburn Convent at No. 8 Hyde Park Place reminding us of the Catholic martyrs who died on the gallows at Tyburn.

3. St Giles-in-the Fields

St Giles is a slightly run-down remnant of old London, which lies in the immediate shadow of the Centre Point building in Charing Cross Road. The Angel public house and the notice in front of the adjoining church of St Giles, rebuilt in 1733 on the site of two previous buildings, are reminders that this was the place of some of the cruellest executions to take place in London. It was a rural place of execution, before being superseded by Tyburn.

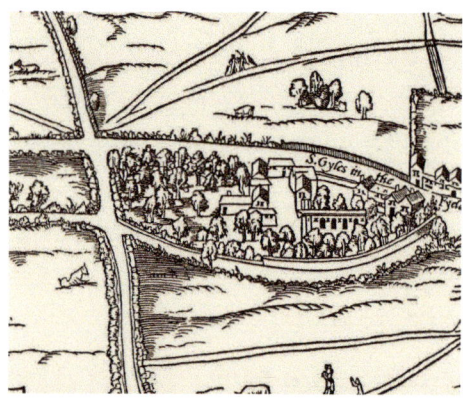

The settlement of St Giles-in-the-Fields on the 'Agas' map of *c.* 1560.

St Giles-in-the-Fields in 1658.

Origins as a Place of Execution

It is probable that its origins as a place of execution began when criminals were no longer hanged at 'the Elms' in Smithfield. A nineteenth-century London history comments that, 'When criminals ceased to be executed at the Elms in Smithfield, or, as some say, at a much earlier date, a gallows was set up near the northwest corner of the wall of the hospital...'

The hospital was in the immediate vicinity of the church, which is still splendidly preserved. The first mention of an execution here dates from 1413 when Sir John Oldcastle, a member of the sect known as Lollards, which met nearby in the fields adjoining St Giles Hospital, was executed by being hanged in chains over a slow fire.

After St Giles ceased to be a place of execution, its role in London's ritual of death continued. Being on the processional route from Newgate to Tyburn, the victims stopped at the Bowl public house for their final glass of ale. We are told that

> Parton, in his *History of the Parish*, published in 1822, makes mention of a public-house bearing the sign of 'The Bowl', which stood between the end of St Giles's, High Street, and Hog Lane ... The 'Bowl' would appear to have been succeeded by the 'Angel', or to have had a rival in that inn. At all events, in 1873, the City Press reported that another memorial of ancient London was about to pass away, namely, the 'Angel' Inn, at St Giles's, the 'half-way house' on the road to Tyburn – the house at which Jack Ketch and the criminal who was about to expiate his offence on the scaffold were wont to stop on their way to the gallows for a 'last glass'. Mr. W. T. Purkiss, the proprietor, however, was prevailed upon to stay the work of demolition for a time.

The Angel, formerly the Bowl, where victims stopped for refreshments on their way to the gallows at Tyburn.

St Giles-in-the-Fields Church. The gallows stood near the main door.

Location of the St Giles Gallows

In the June 1856 edition of *The Gentleman's Magazine,* a contributor noted that the site of the gallows at St Giles-in-the-Fields was 'near the north-west corner of the wall of Saint Giles's Hospital, which was not far from the front entrance of the present church; it was removed to this spot early in the fifteenth century from the Elms in Smithfield'.

None of the early London maps depict these gallows, although the comment that they were 'not far from the front entrance of the present church' allows a close approximation of their location. When Oldcastle (Lord Cobham) was executed,

> A new gallows was put up for that special occasion. But Lord Cobham was not the only distinguished person who here paid the last penalty of the law. St Giles Pound was the site of execution during the reign of Elizabeth for some of the Babbington Plot conspirators, though Babington himself suffered at Lincoln's Inn Fields.

Executions at St Giles

Sir John Oldcastle, or Lord Cobham, perished here in 1417 – the first execution we know of at this site. Cobham who was accused of Lollardism, a political and religious movement inspired by John Wyclif, which sought the reformation and cleansing of the Catholic Church. It was judged treasonable by Parliament, and Cobham was imprisoned in the Tower for his beliefs. He escaped, led an insurrection with the aim of capturing the king, but was once more arrested. He was brought to St Giles from the Tower, where he had been held on a hurdle with his hands pinioned behind his back.

On arriving at St Giles, Oldcastle was assisted from the hurdle. He knelt down and offered prayers, as was customary, for the forgiveness of all, including his enemies. He then turned to the assembled crowds and warned them to obey the scriptures and the laws of God. Iron chains were attached to his waist and he was raised aloft then suspended over a fire, which gave Oldcastle an agonizingly slow death. He 'praised the name of the Lord so long as his life lasted', but the clergy attending the execution forbade the crowd to pray for Oldcastle:

> The priests and friars stood by the while, forbidding the people to pray for one who, as he was departing 'not in the obedience of their Pope', was about to be plunged into fiercer flames than those in which they beheld him consuming. The martyr, now near his end, lifting up his voice for the last time, commended his soul into the hands of God, and 'so departed hence most Christianly'. 'Thus' adds the chronicler, 'rested this valiant Christian knight, Sir John Oldcastle, under the Altar of God, which is Jesus Christ; among that godly company which, in the kingdom of patience, suffered great tribulation, with the death of their bodies, for his faithful word and testimony; abiding there with them the fulfilling of their whole number, and the full restoration of his elect.'

What Remains to be Seen?
The main entrance of the present church marks the approximate location of the gallows, and there is a large notice by the railings in the churchyard that mentions some of the executions and the names of those buried in the churchyard. The Angel public house, formerly the Bowl, is a few yards away.

4. Newgate

Newgate Gaol, throughout its 800-year history, was renowned for all that was inhumane in early London society. It was a holding prison for those awaiting trial and punishment and in the manner of the lunatic asylum, Bedlam, was also a source of entertainment for the eighteenth-century upper classes as a place to visit and observe the inmates. After Tyburn gallows were abolished in 1783, public hangings continued at Newgate until 1868 when public executions were abolished altogether.

Diagonally opposite the site of the prison, in Giltspur Street, is St Sepulchre's Church. When executions were still at Tyburn, the condemned received nosegays outside the church, mounted a cart containing their own coffin, and began the near 3-mile journey to Tyburn and the scaffold. Sometimes the mob that travelled with the carts and lined the route would be so dense that the prisoners would have to dismount and walk.

The gaol, which was closed in 1902 and demolished in 1904, was on the site of a Roman gateway, the remains of which were revealed when digging foundations for the Central Criminal Court early in the twentieth century. The prison was synonymous with squalor and corruption, from the jailers that charged prisoners for the necessities of life, to the conditions that meant that many who slept in filthy straw were more likely to die of disease than on the scaffold.

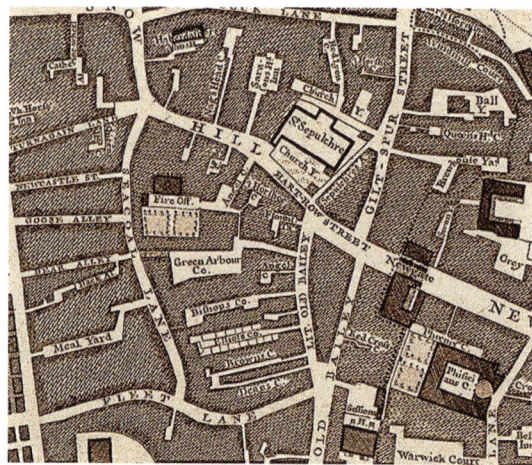
Detail from Rocque's map of 1746, showing the Newgate Prison area.

Origins of Newgate

City Corporation records contain references to committals to Newgate dating from 1218. It is possible that a description, from around 1188, by William Fitzstephen, clerk to Thomas Becket, refers to Newgate. He relates, 'On the west are two towers very strongly fortified with the high and great wall of the city, having seven double gates.'

Stow tells us that in 1241 the Jews of Norwich 'were constrained to pay twenty thousand marks, at two terms in the year, or else be kept perpetual prisoners in Newgate', and that in 1326, Robert Baldock, the king's chancellor, was put in Newgate. More tellingly in regard to the appalling conditions and disease there, Stow says that in 1414 'the gaolers of Newgate and Ludgate died, and prisoners in Newgate to the number of sixty-four'. Poor conditions for prisoners was a feature during its entire existence, as are references to bequests with which to sustain inmates. From 1422, license was granted to 'John Coventry, Jenken Carpenter, and William Grove, executors to Richard Whittington, to re-edify the gaol of Newgate, which they did with his goods.' It was with Whittington's bequest that the prison was rebuilt, but if the intention was to improve conditions, it was a failure. The prison was destroyed in the Great Fire of 1666 and then rebuilt and extended in 1667.

The Horror of Newgate

From a pamphlet published in 1724 and written by B. L of Twickenham, who 'had clearly spent considerable time within the jail'. 'At the entrance to the prison was a lodge where prisoners are first received, and where they are fettered if the cause of their imprisonment require it.' It notes that all prisoners were manacled unless 'a financial bargain' had been struck.

> These manacles were on both the hands and feet, and were heavily made. If it were known to the jailers that the prisoners had the control of money they were kept on until 'easement' had been bought. If, on the other hand it was self-evident that the unfortunate person was penniless and without friends able to secure good treatment,

he was either unchained or left manacled, at the humour of his jailers. Extortion was practised in Newgate quite up to the middle of the nineteenth century. Of course, by that period it had been so checked that jailers proceeded very cautiously, while, as more humane principles gradually ruled the prison, the pretences for extortion became less.

Worse than extortion was carried out in Newgate. Reinforcing an image of the place, as an early chamber of horrors, the body parts of those that had been sentenced to be hanged, drawn and quartered were delivered to the jail for post-execution disposal.

The Condemned and Newgate Chapel

In 1810 there were over fifty persons awaiting execution in the condemned cells, three or four kept together.

Dickens makes reference to the custom of the condemned being forced to sit in the chapel, at prayer, with their own coffin beside them: 'At one time – and at no distant period either – the coffins of the men about to be executed, were placed in that pew, upon the seat by their side, during the whole service. It may seem incredible, but it is true…'

Among those sentenced to death were children. As late as 1833 a nine-year-old child who stole some paint from a shop, having poked a stick through the window, was sentenced to death, but the sentence commuted to detention in a penitentiary. The child would have stood in front of a judge, who would have with all the solemn paraphernalia of the law condemned him to be hanged until dead.

Newgate Chapel in 1809, showing the death sermon being read to those about to be executed. Note the coffin situated in front of the prisoners and the spectators in the gallery.

One of the Newgate condemned cells in which three or four persons would be kept together. Dickens described them as 'stone dungeons'.

The Condemned
Women sentenced to death were not segregated, so were mixed in appalling conditions with other women, and often children, until they were taken away for execution. Their final hours would be spent in one of the condemned cells.

Attending an execution at Newgate
An account, related by a Captain Shaw, witness to one of the last executions outside Newgate in 1864 cuts through the often righteous, voyeuristic accounts common to the *Newgate Calendar* and describes the events in the context of an awakening realisation that public executions stood in total defiance of every precept of a country that believed in its own humanity. Shaw writes how hanging as a deterrent to crime can be seen to have little effect on those attending:

> The scene on the night preceding a public execution afforded a study of the dark side of nature not to be obtained under any other circumstances. Here was to be seen the lowest scum of London densely packed together as far as the eye could see, and estimated by *The Times* at not less than 20,000. Across the entire front of Newgate heavy barricades of stout timber traversed the streets in every direction, erected as a precaution against the pressure of the crowd ... As the crowd increased wholesale highway robberies were of most frequent occurrence; and victims in the hands of some two or three desperate ruffians were as far from help as though divided by a continent from the battalions of police surrounding the scaffold.

Shaw went on:

> The scene that met one's view on pulling up the windows ... and looking out on the black night sky and its blacker accompaniments baffles description. A surging mass, with here and there a flickering torch, rolled and roared before one; above this weird scene arose the voices of men and women shouting, singing, blaspheming, and, as the night advanced and the liquid gained firmer mastery, it seemed as if hell had

An execution in front of the Debtor's Door, Newgate, from an 1809 print.

> delivered up its victims. To approach the window was a matter of danger; volleys of mud immediately saluted one, accompanied by more blaspheming and shouts of defiance. It was difficult to believe one was in the centre of a civilised capital that vaunted its religion and yet meted out justice in such a form.

He captured the dark atmosphere that took place outside the old building in the early hours of the morning of execution. At 4 a.m. workmen appeared,

> immediately followed by a rumbling sound, and one realised that the scaffold was being dragged round. A grim, square, box-like apparatus was now distinctly visible, as it slowly backed against the debtors 'door' [the door through which the condemned appeared was one storey above the pavement]. Lights now flickered about the scaffold – the workmen fixing the cross-beams and uprights. Every stroke of the hammer must have vibrated through the condemned cells, and warned the wakeful occupants that their time was nearly come.

Shaw then described the activity that took place in and around the prison kitchen,

> Meanwhile, a little unpretending door was gently opened; this was the 'debtor's door', and led directly through the kitchen on to the scaffold. The kitchen on these occasions was turned into a temporary mausoleum and draped with tawdry black hangings, which concealed the pots and pans, and produced an effect supposed to be more in keeping with the solemn occasion.

Shaw tells us that, an 'old and decrepit man' made his appearance. This was the executioner, Calcraft, who then proceeded to test the drop. By 7.30 a.m. the street theatre was almost due to begin:

> The tolling of St Sepulchre's bell about 7.30am announced the approach of the hour of execution; meanwhile a steady rain was falling, though without diminishing the

ever-increasing crowd. As far as the eye could reach was a sea of human faces. Roofs, windows, church-rails, and empty vans – all were pressed into service, and tightly packed with human beings. The rain had made the drop slippery, and necessitated precautions on behalf of the living if not of those appointed to die, so sand was thrown over a portion. The sand was for the benefit of the 'ordinary', the minister of religion, who was to offer the dying consolation at 8 am, and breakfast at 9.

Then came the procession of the condemned through the kitchen. Shaw describes the condemned as a cadaverous mob, securely pinioned, and literally as white as marble.

As they reached the platform a halt was necessary as each was placed one by one immediately under the hanging chains. At the end of these chains were hooks which were eventually attached to the hemp round the neck of each wretch. The concluding ceremonies did not take long, considering how feeble the aged hangman was. A white cap was first placed over every face, then the ankles were strapped together, and finally the fatal noose was put around every neck, and the end attached to the hooks. ... The silence was now awful. One felt one's heart literally in one's mouth, and found oneself involuntarily saying, 'They could be saved yet – yet – yet,' and then a thud that vibrated through the street announced that the felons were launched into eternity.

In the seconds and minutes after the trap had opened:

One's eyes were glued to the spot and, fascinated by the awful sight, not a detail escaped one. Calcraft, meanwhile, apparently not satisfied with his handiwork, seized hold of one poor wretch's feet, and pressing on them for some seconds with all his weight, passed from one to another with hideous composure...

After the multitude had allowed the statutory hour to pass during which the bodies remained suspended Shaw informs us that the 'drunken again took up their ribald songs, conspicuous amongst which was one that had done duty pretty well through the night, and ended with "Calcraft, Calcraft, he's the man." The latter is reminiscent of a scene at a football match, following a well-executed goal. The show was now almost over with the exception of the removal of the bodies.

When St Sepulchre chimed 9 o clock, 'Calcraft, rubbing his lips, again appeared, and, producing a clasp knife, proceeded to hug the various bodies in rotation with one arm whilst with the other he severed the several ropes. It required two slashes of the feeble old arm to complete this final ceremony, and then the heads fell with a flop on the old man's breast...' Calcraft staggered under the weight and proceeded to 'jam' the bodies into their awaiting coffins.

Disposal of Felons' Bodies
At Newgate the deceased were buried under paving stones within the jail; the same paving stones over which they had walked on their final journey to the gallows.

Dead Man's Walk in 1902. The deceased felons were buried under the paving stones.

What There is to See

Of Newgate itself there are some remnants in much of the original brick of the Old Bailey. There are cells beneath the Viaduct pub, almost opposite, and there is a plaque marking the site of the jail on the wall of the Old Bailey itself. The Museum of London possesses cell doors belonging to the prison, while the debtor's door, in front of which the executions took place, is now in America.

In the immediate vicinity was until recently the Magpie & Stump public house at No.18 Old Bailey, which stood on the site of an older pub of the same name. It once rented out its upstairs rooms to provide a grandstand view of the executions immediately opposite. Opposite is now a new development which has obliterated this well-known pub.

Newgate Prison from a photograph shortly before its demolition in 1904.

The Old Bailey sits on the site of Newgate Gaol and was built using much of the original stone as Newgate Prison.

A public execution at Newgate in the late eighteenth century.

This photograph is taken from the approximate location of the Debtor's Door, where the gallows stood. St Sepulchre is in the background with the former Newgate Prison on the right.

St Sepulchre

St Sepulchre-without-Newgate Church, the ancient but much rebuilt church for Newgate Prison is close to the Old Bailey at the junction of Holborn Viaduct and Giltspur Street. It was from outside this church that the condemned began their journey to Tyburn in carts. It was also here that on 20 June 1698 the wall at the corner of the churchyard collapsed on the crowd who pushed too hard against it in their attempt to see six condemned criminals depart for Tyburn. A contemporary account in *The Post Man* gives one person as killed outright, four dying later, and forty injured. St Sepulchre is the church named in the nursery rhyme 'Oranges and Lemons' as the 'bells of Old Bailey.'

The Execution Bell

On display in a glass case on a pillar at the south east end of the nave is the original execution bell, which from 1605 was rung at midnight outside the condemned cell.

The clerk of St Sepulchre, who traditionally rang the bell, travelled from the church to the prison by way of an underground tunnel.

5. Charing Cross

Location of Execution Site

There are a number of references to a gallows at Charing Cross. The Braun and Hogenberg map of London from *c.* 1560 depicts gallows almost directly in front of today's National Gallery, to the south of Nelson's Column.

Henry Machyn, a funeral director who kept a diary of London events between 1550 and 1563, makes frequent reference to executions at Charing Cross:

> The 25th day of October was hanged at Charing Cross a Spaniard who killed a servant of Sir George Gifford, which was slain with-out Temple Bar. The 26th day of April was carried from the Marshalsea (Prison) in a cart through London unto Charing Cross to the gallows, and there hanged three men for robbing of certain Spaniards of treasure of gold out of the abbey of Westminster.
>
> The 29th day of April was cut down off the gallows a man that was hanged the 26th day of April, a poulter's servant that was one of them that did robbed the Spaniard within-in Westminster Abbey, and he hanged in a gown of tawny fryse and a doublet of tawny taffeta and a pair of fine hose lined with sarsenet, and after buried under the gallows, rayllyng against the pope and the mass, and hanged 4 days.

Above: Trafalgar Square by Canaletto, *c.* 1750. Note the Charles I bronze statue to the right where regicides were executed.

Below right: A pamphlet devoted to 'The arraignment of John Selman', accused of theft in the King's Chapel. He was executed at Charing Cross in 1612.

Left: The statue of Charles I on the southern part of Trafalgar Square, placed there in 1675 on the site of the execution of the regicides and looking towards the Banqueting House where Charles I was beheaded.

There was to be no peace for the poulterer's assistance:

> The 7th day of May was taken out of his grave the same man that was buried beside the gallows at Charing Cross, a poulterer, and burned beside the gallows.

The Dying Speech of John Selman at His Place of Execution, Charing Cross, 7 January 1612

> I am come (as you see) patiently to offer up the sweet, and dear sacrifice of my life, a life, which I have gracelessly abused, and by the unruly course thereof, made my death a scandal to my kindred and acquaintance: I have consumed fortune's gifts in riotous companies, wasted my good name in the purchase of goods unlawfully gotten, and now ending my days in too late repentance, I am placed in the rank of reprobates, which the rusty canker of time must needs turn to oblivion. I stand here as shame's example, ready to be spewed out of the Commonwealth. I confess I have known too much, performed more, but consented to most: I have been the only corruption of many ripe witted youth, and leader of them to confusion. Pardon me God, for that is now a burden to my conscience, wash it away sweet Creator, that I may spotless enter into thy glorious kingdom. Whereupon being demanded, if he would discover any of his fraternity, for the good of the Commonwealth or not: Answered, that he had already left the names of divers notorious malefactors in writing behind him, which he thought sufficient. So he requested the quietness of conscience that his soul might depart without molestation. For (quoth he) I have deserved death long before this time, and deservedly now I suffer death. The offense I die for, was high presumption, a fact done even in the Kings Majesty's presence, even in the Church of God, in the time of divine Service, and the celebration of the Sacred Communion, for which if forgiveness may descend from God's tribunal Throne, with penitence of heart I desire it, all which being spoken, he patiently left this world for another life.

In the annals of executions Charing Cross is best known as being the place of execution for the regicides who had signed the death warrant of Charles I in 1649. It was appropriately close to the Banqueting Hall in Whitehall, where the king had died and the present statue of Charles I on horseback marks the spot, where the regicides met their own deaths.

Execution of Thomas Harrison, Regicide.

Major-General Thomas Harrison played a key role in the execution of Charles I and was responsible for bringing the king from captivity at Hurst Castle for trial in London. He was also a signatory to the king's death warrant. In order to restore confidence and heal a divided country, Charles II, on his return in 1660, issued an amnesty known as the Declaration of Breda, outlining the conditions in which he would return to the throne (written on 4 April 1660); he declared that,

> We do grant a free and general pardon ... to all our subjects, of what degree or quality so ever, who, within forty days after the publishing hereof, shall lay hold upon this

our grace and favour, and shall, by any public act, declare their doing so, and that they return to the loyalty and obedience of good subjects; excepting only such persons as shall hereafter be excepted by Parliament...

The subsequent Indemnity and Oblivion Act of the same year excluded the regicides, of whom Thomas Harrison was one. Harrison couldn't possibly hope to escape the ultimate sentence at his trial and thus stood bravely by his beliefs and principles. On 13 October 1660 Harrison was taken from Newgate to Charing Cross and was hanged, drawn and quartered.

Pepys's diary entry for that day illustrates the almost casual manner that judicial death was observed: after having attended one of the grimmest forms of public execution, he immediately continues his social plans for the day:

To my Lord's in the morning, where I met with Captain Cuttance, but my Lord not being up I went out to Charing Cross, to see Major-General Harrison hanged, drawn, and quartered; which was done there, he looking as cheerful as any man could do in that condition. He was presently cut down, and his head and heart shown to the people, at which there was great shouts of joy. It is said, that he said that he was sure to come shortly at the right hand of Christ to judge them that now had judged him; and that his wife do expect his coming again. Thus it was my chance to see the King beheaded at White Hall, and to see the first bloodshed in revenge for the blood of the King at Charing Cross. From thence to my Lord's, and took Captain Cuttance and Mr. Sheply to the Sun Tavern, and did give them some oysters ... Within all the afternoon setting up shelves in my study. At night to bed.

The magnificently titled *An Exact and Impartial Accompt Of the Indictment, Arraignment, Tryal, and Judgment (according to Law) of Twenty Nine Regicides, The Murtherers of His Late Sacred Majesty Of Most Glorious Memory* published in London in 1679, summarised the fate of a number of the regicides:

Thus having given the Reader a most impartial view of every Passage occurring in this so solemn and legal Indictment, Arraignment, Trial, and Condemnation of these twenty nine black Regicides, with their several Pleas and Defences in their own words. It may be also some additional satisfaction, to let the Reader know the time and manner of such of them who were according to the Sentence Executed. For their last Discourses and Prayers, as they were made in a Croud, and therefore not possible to be taken exactly ; so it was thought fit rather to say nothing, than give an untrue account thereof ; chusing rather to appear lame, than to be supported with imperfect assistances.

According to the *State Trials and Proceedings*, Harrison showed no fear:

The Sheriff came that morning that he was to die, and told him, that in half an hour he must be gone; he answered that he was ready, and would not have him stay at all on his account. But the sheriff left him to stay a little longer, and in the meantime, he was longing for the sheriff's coming, and all his friends judged he was in haste to be gone, and said, he was going about a great work for the Lord that day; and that his support was, that his sufferings were upon the account of Jehovah, the Lord of Hosts ... He parted with his wife and friends with great joy and chearfulness.

On arriving at Charing Cross he hugged his servant and 'went up the ladder with an undaunted countenance; from whence he spake to the multitude...' Just how important one's behaviour at the scaffold was, and how every minutiae was noted can be seen from an observation of a slight tremble in his hand and one of his legs. On noting that this has been seen, Harrison, during the course of his speech beneath the gallows said, 'Gentlemen, by reason of some scoffing that I do hear, I judge that some do think I am afraid to die, by the shaking I have in my hands and knees; I tell you, no, but it is by reason of much blood I have lost in the wars, and many wounds I have received in my body, which caused this shaking and weakness in my nerves...' His speech continued at some length and the sheriff had to remind him of the shortness of time. *State Trials and Proceedings* notes that on finishing he was 'turned off, and was cut down, alive, for after his body was opened, he mounted himself, and gave the executioner a box on the ear.' Ludlow commented that the sentence was carried out in a barbaric manner. The *Exact and Impartial Accompt of the Indictment* volume fills in some detail:

> On Saturday the 13 October 1660, betwixt nine and ten of the clock in the Morning, Mr. Tho. Harrison, or, Major General Harrison, according to this sentence, was upon a Hurdle drawn from Newgate to the place called Charing-Cross; where within certain Rails lately there made, a Gibbet was erected, and he hanged with his face looking towards the Banqueting-house at Whitehall, (the place where our late Sovereign of eternal memory was sacrificed) being half dead, he was cut down by the common Executioner, his Privy Members cut off before his eyes, his Bowels burned, his Head severed from his Body, and his Body divided into Quarters, which were returned back to Newgate upon the same Hurdle that carried it. His Head is since set on a Pole on the top of the South-East end of Westminster-Hall, looking towards London. The Quarters of his Body are in like manner exposed upon some of the City Gates.
>
> Monday following, being the 15th October, about the same hour, Mr. John Carew was carried in the like manner to the same place of Execution; where having suffered like pains, his Quarters were also returned to Newgate on the same Hurdle which carried him. His Majesty was pleased to give, upon intercession made by his Friends, his Body to be buried.

Of Carew, *State Trials and Proceedings* tell us that he was cheerful all the way to the gibbet, 'setting forth his joy in the Lord.' On the ladder he made a lengthy speech, and again the sheriff interrupted suggesting that he now pray. After the completion of his prayers he bade farewell to his friends telling them that 'we part with much joy in our souls.' He was then executed in the manner of Harrison. Evelyn's diary entry notes that 'Scot, Scroop, Cook, and Jones, suffered for reward of their iniquities at Charing Cross, in sight of the place where they put to death their natural prince, and in the presence of the King, his son, whom they also sought to kill.' He writes, 'I saw not their execution, but met their quarters, mangled and cut, and reeking, as they were brought from the gallows in baskets on the hurdle.'

Francis Hacker and Daniel Axtel probably on account of the public backlash against the cruelty being shown in the commission of the sentences were executed at Tyburn:

> Mr. Francis Hacker and Mr. Daniel Axtel, were on Friday 19th October, about the same time of the morning, drawn on one Hurdle from Newgate to Tiburn, and there both Hanged; Mr. Axtel was Quartered, and returned back, and disposed as the former; but the Body of Mr. Hacker was, by his Majesties great favour, given entire to his Friends, and buried.

6. Old and New Palace Yards, Westminster

Executions at Old and New Palace Yards

New and Old Palace Yards were part and parcel of the old Palace of Westminster, now the Houses of Parliament. They still exist but in a different form within the present building's complex. Old Palace Yard lies west of the St Stephens entrance; to the House of Lords new Palace Yard is a small garden on top of the MP's car park to the north of Westminster Hall. The Hall, originally built in 1097 to 1099 but given its famous hammer beam roof in 1399, is the oldest part of the palace. It was the setting for

New Palace Yard. It was a place of punishment from the fourteenth century onwards.

Old Palace Yard.

Inset: Old Palace Yard. Executions would have taken place in the central area.

the trials of William Wallace (1305), Sir Thomas More (1535), the Gunpowder Plot conspirators (1606) and Charles I (1649).

At New Palace Yard a Puritan attorney, John Stubs, along with his servant and Robert Page, had their hands cut off for libelling Elizabeth I. Not long afterwards a William Parry was hanged, drawn and quartered for treason. In 1612, Lord Sanquire was hanged here, in front of Westminster Hall for murder.

At Old Palace Yard died some Gunpowder Plot conspirators, while others were despatched at St Paul's Churchyard. Sir Walter Raleigh was executed here after many years of imprisonment in the Tower.

The Execution of Sir Walter Raleigh at Old Palace Yard, Westminster

Sir Walter Raleigh (1552–1618) first tasted prison life when Elizabeth I discovered that he had secretly married one of her ladies-in-waiting in 1592. He gradually returned to favour but in 1603 was found guilty of intriguing against James I and remained in the Tower of London until 1616. In 1616 he was freed and allowed to lead a search for El Dorado. The expedition was a failure, and upset the Spanish. The Spanish ambassador demanded that James carry out Raleigh's suspended death sentence. Raleigh was being held in the Tower until his execution on 29 October 1618. On that day, it was related,

> It was now near nine, and having declared himself ready he was led to the place of execution, in the Old Palace Yard, by the Sheriffs of London and the Dean of Westminster. A great crowd had assembled, and as many pushed forward to gaze on him, among the rest one venerable old man, whose head was quite bald, came so near that Sir Walter noticed him and inquired if he wanted ought with him; the old man answered, that his only desire was to see him, and to pray God for him: 'I thank thee, my good friend,' said Raleigh, 'and am sorry I am in no case to return thee anything for thy good-will'. 'But,' added he, looking at his bald head, 'here, take this nightcap', removing that which he wore beneath his hat, 'thou hast more need of it now than I'.

Shortly, in a very leisured, stately, and gentlemanly manner, Raleigh reached the scaffold:

> The people pressed him so much that, faint from sickness, he had nearly swooned away before he reached the scaffold, which was erected in front of the parliament-house ... On coming to the steps he recovered, mounted them easily, and saluted those who stood near with the same graceful courtesy which usually distinguished his manners. Proclamation was then made for silence, and Raleigh standing up, although very feeble, addressed those around him. His last words have been transmitted to us by several persons who were present, and we read them almost exactly as he delivered them...

Raleigh was concerned, that not feeling well, his weakness will be taken to be a sign of fear. He made it clear to those around him, it was not fear that caused him to shake:

> I have had for these two days past, two fits of an ague. Yesterday I was, notwithstanding, taken out of my bed in one of my fits, and whether I shall escape it this day or not I cannot tell. If therefore, you perceive any weakness in me, I beseech you ascribe it to my sickness rather than to myself.

There then followed a lengthy vindication of his innocence, read from pre-prepared notes. So weak from illness was he that in the middle of his speech he was compelled to sit down. His words were spoken 'with grace and animation'. Drawing to a close, he then embraced the many assembled lords who stood with him on the scaffold and asked them to ensure that no defamatory matter would be published after his death.

Comfort on the Scaffold

The morning was cold and the sheriff suggested to Raleigh that he come down off the scaffold and warm himself in front of a fire before saying his prayers. Raleigh replied, 'No, good Mr Sheriff, let us despatch, for within this quarter of an hour my ague will come upon me, and if I be not dead before that, mine enemies shall say I quake for fear.'

The Execution

After saying prayers Raleigh arose and said that he was now 'going to God!' The scaffold was cleared of unnecessary personnel in preparation. Raleigh took off his gown and doublet and then asked the executioner to show him the axe. There was a pause as there was an initial reluctance to do this, possibly in case it would cause him to show fear. It was usual for the axe itself to be hidden. He repeated his request. 'I prithee let me see it. Dost thou think I am afraid of it? Running his fingers along the edge of the blade he commented to the sheriff that the axe 'tis a sharp medicine, but a sound cure for all diseases.' Kneeling down he prayed and requested those around him to pray for him. He then stood up again and examined the block 'laying himself down to fit it to his neck, and to choose the easiest and most decent attitude...' He stood up yet again, declaring himself ready, at which point the executioner came forward and

The execution of Sir Walter Raleigh.

asked Raleigh's forgiveness. He then said that when he gave the signal, the executioner should 'fear nothing and strike home.' He then again lay down and put his head on the block at which point the executioner asked if he could 'face to the east'. It is likely that this was to ensure that he was not facing the executioner. He prayed further and gave the signal for the executioner to strike, but for some reason the executioner hesitated. Raleigh then partially raised his head saying 'what dost thou fear? Strike, man!'

Raleigh's Head

After being displayed to the crowd, Raleigh's head was placed in a red bag, over which his velvet nightgown was thrown and the whole being carried to a mourning coach waiting nearby. The remains were conveyed to Lady Raleigh who had the head embalmed and preserved in a case. The remainder of Raleigh's body was buried in an unmarked grave near the altar of St Margaret's Church, Westminster.

His wife survived him by twenty-nine years. After her death, his son Carew kept the head, and on his death it was buried with him in St Margaret's, and later exhumed, along with the head to be buried in St Mary's Church, West Horsley, Surrey, near the family seat which is not far from Guildford. Raleigh's body lies in St Margaret's Church where there is a memorial plaque.

The Church of St Mary in West Horsley dates from 1030. It contains well preserved thirteenth-century wall paintings. Raleigh's head and the remains of his son Carew lie unmarked beneath the floor of the chapel, behind the organ. A letter written by William Nicholas, who owned Raleigh's former estate in the eighteenth century and whose remains reside in the chapel, records that 'the head he saw dug up there in 1703, from the side of a grave where a Carew Raleigh had been buried, was that of Sir Walter Raleigh; there being no bones of a body to it, nor room for any, the rest of that side of the grave being firm chalk.'

St Mary's Church, West Horsley near Guildford holds the head of Sir Walter Raleigh.

Background to the Gunpowder Plot

The plot to blow up the Houses of Parliament and reinstate Roman Catholicism as the country's religion was aborted on 5 November 1605 when one of the conspirators, Guy Fawkes, was discovered in the cellars of Parliament with thirty-six barrels of gunpowder. The trials of the conspirators began on 27 January 1606, exciting much contemporary comment. The subsequent executions of the eight traitors, sentenced to be hanged, drawn and quartered began a matter of weeks later and were gruesome in the extreme. Guy Fawkes had been tortured to such an extent that the signature on his confession is barely legible, and he had to be helped up the steps of the ladder at his execution. The four to die in Old Palace Yard were Thomas Winter, Rookwood, Keyes, and Guy Fawkes.

State Trials and Proceedings deals briefly with the fate of the Westminster victims:

> The next day, being Friday, were drawn from the Tower, to the Old Palace in Westminster, Thomas Winter, Rookwood, Keyes, and Fawkes, where Winter, first being brought to the scaffold, made little speech, but seeming after a sort, as it were, sorry for his offence, and yet crossing himself, as though these were words ... went up to the Ladder, and after a swing or two with a halter, to the quartering block was drawn, and there quickly despatched.

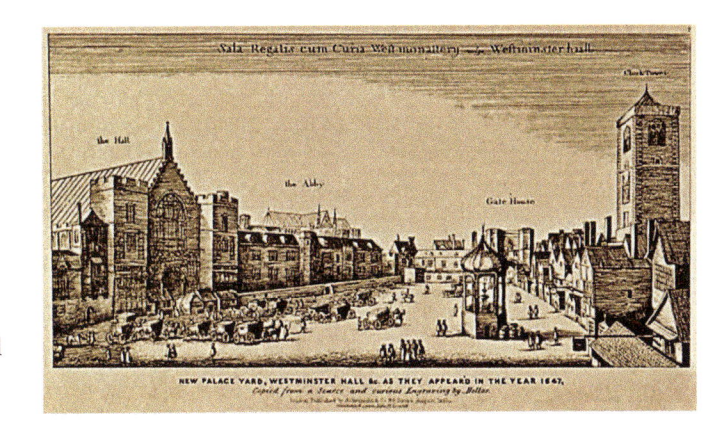

View of Westminster Hall and New Palace Yard, c. 1647.

It is clear that only two swings on the gallows was a deliberate act so disembowelling and quartering would be carried out while Winter was alive and conscious. The next to be executed was Rockwood,

> who made a speech of some longer time, confessing his offence to God, in seeking to shed blood ... But last of all, to mar all the pottage with one filthy weed ... he prayed God to make the king a catholick, otherwise a papist ... protesting to die in his idolatary, a Romish Catholick, he went up the ladder, and, hanging till he was almost dead, was drawn to the block, where he gave his last gasp.

Keyes who followed showed no repentance and 'went stoutly up the ladder' off which he jumped attempting to break his own neck, but the halter broke and he fell to the ground. Rather than hang him again, the executioner took him straight to the block where he was quartered. *State Trials and Proceedings* tells us that,

> Last of all came the great devil of Fawkes ... who should have put fire to the powder. His body was weak with torture and sickness, and he was scarcely able to go up the ladder, but yet with much ado, by the help of the hangman, went high enough to break his neck with the fall: who made no long speech, but, after a sort, seeming to be sorry for his offence, asked a kind of forgiveness of the king and the state for his blood intent; and, with his crosses and his idle ceremonies, made his end upon the gallows and the block, to the great joy of the beholders, that the land was ended of so wicked a villainy.

English Civil War Executions, 9 March 1649

After the execution of Charles I in 1649, a number of his commanders and supporters were captured, tried at Westminster Hall, and sentenced to die all on the same day Friday 9 March 1649.

At 10 a.m. the three to die, the Duke of Hamilton (born 1606), the Earl of Holland (born around 1590), and Arthur, Lord Capel (born 1604) were summoned from St James's Palace under armed sedan to the home of Sir Thomas Cotton in Westminster

The Duke of Hamilton (1606–49), Royalist and politician.

where they were allowed to remain for prayers and conversation for around two hours before being summoned to the scaffold. The executions took place on a scaffold in New Palace Yard, 'over against the great hall gate, in the site of the place where the high court of justice formerly sat, the hall doors being open...'

Duke of Hamilton

Hamilton went first and said goodbye to his friends. On the scaffold he justified his actions, and entered into an in-depth religious dialogue with his chaplain, after which he turned to the executioner and said, 'I shall say a very short prayer to my God, while I lay down there; and when I stretch out my hand, my right hand, then, sir, do your duty; and I do freely forgive you, and so I do all the world.' The duke then lay on the block and for a short while prayed, then stretched out his right hand and the executioner removed his head with one blow of the axe. Hamilton's servants immediately wrapped the head in a crimson scarf, and placed it in the coffin that waited on the scaffold, along with the body. It was then taken to Sir John Hamilton's house 'at the Mews'. The sheriff's guard then immediately sent for the Earl of Holland.

The Earl of Holland

Henry Rich, 1st Earl of Holland, was so incensed that he was brought to the block. He had been promised a pardon when he had surrendered to the Parliamentarians, but was tried and sentenced to death. By the time he was led to the scaffold he was so ill that it was believed had he not been executed, he would have died in a matter of days. The account of his execution suggests a man uneasy with the protocols of the scaffold:

Holland (To the executioner): Which is the way of lying? (He is shown, and then walks

Henry Rich, 1st Earl of Holland.

to the front of the scaffold to address the crowd. He blesses them and wishes them happiness. He then turns to the executioner)
Holland: How must I lie? I know not.
Executioner: Lie down flat upon your belly.
Holland then lay down and spoke to the executioner.
Holland: Must I lie closer?
Executioner: Yes, and backwarder.
Holland: I will tell you when you shall strike. (He then prayed whilst lying with his head on the block. He lifted up his head). Where is the man? (He sees the executioner standing next to him). Stay while I give the sign.

Holland then stretched out his hand catching the executioner by surprise. He had to shout Now! Now! twice before the axe struck.

Arthur, Lord Capel
Dr Morley, Bishop of Winchester, wrote to Edward Symonds, Capel's chaplain informing him that he was

> there at the time assigned ... But he was to have an agony before his passion; and that was the parting with his wife, eldest son, son-in-law, two of his uncles, and Sir Thomas Corbet, especially the parting with his most dear lady; which was the saddest spectacle that I ever beheld ... in blessing the young lord, he commanded him never to revenge his death, though it should be in his power. The like he said unto his Lady ... After this, with much adoe I persuaded his wife and the rest to be gone: and then being all alone with me, he said 'Doctor, the hardest part of my work in this world, is now past'.

The bishop went with Capel to Sir Robert Cotton's house. He says in the letter that he was not allowed to go on the scaffold with him. On being escorted to the scaffold Capel doffed his cap to people on both sides of the crowd. On mounting the scaffold he

Arthur Capel, 1st Baron Capel (1604–49).

was 'greeted' by the Parliamentary minder, Lieutenant-Colonel Beecher who asked him if he had come with his chaplain, to which Capel replied he had not as he had already taken leave of him. Capel was surrounded by weeping servants and asked Beecher if he should make his speech with his hat off, the answer to which was in the affirmative. At the end of a short speech he turned around looking for the executioner who was not at this time on the scaffold and asked 'which is the gentleman, which is the man?' To which he was answered 'He is coming.'

Capel: Stay, I must pull off my doublet first and my waistcoat

The executioner stepped onto the scaffold

Capel: Oh my friend! Pr'ythee come hither

The executioner knelt down and asked Capel's forgiveness

Capel: I forgive thee, but I shall pray God to give thee all grace for a better life. There is five pounds for thee, and truly, for my clothes, and those things, if there be any due to you for it, you shall be fully recompensed: but I desire my body may not be stripped here, and no body to take notice of my body but my own servants. Look you, friend, this I shall desire of you, that when I lie down, you would give me a time for a particular short prayer.

Lieu. Col. Beecher: Make your own sign my lord

Capel: Stay a little. Which side do you stand upon? Stay I think I should lay my hands forward that way (pointing forward to the right)

Executioner: Yes

Capel: God almighty bless all his people: God almighty staunch all this blood: God almighty staunch staunch staunch this issue of blood; this will do the business. God almighty find out another way to do it.

Capel then turned to his servant, Baldwin:

Capel: Baldwin I cannot see anything that belongs to my wife; but I desire thee, and beseech her, to rest wholly upon Jesus Christ, to be contented and fully satisfied. Capel then turned to his servants,

Capel: Pray at the moment of striking join your prayers, but make no noise ... it is inconvenient at this time.

Servant: My lord put on your cap.

Capel: Should I, what will that do me good? (He put up his hair) Stay a little, it is as well as it is now. – (turning to the executioner)
Capel: Honest man, I have forgiven thee, therefore strike boldly; from my soul I do it,
A gentleman then turned to speak to Capel.
Capel: Nay, die contented; be quiet, good Mr ----be quiet. (Capel then turned again to the executioner:
Capel: Well, you are ready when I am ready, are you not ... (Capel then stretched out his hands) then pray standoff, gentlemen.
He then walked to the front of the scaffold and speaking to the crowd:
Capel: Gentlemen, tho I doubt not of it, yet I think it convenient to ask of you, that you would all join in prayers with me, that God would mercifully receive my soul, and that for his alone mercies in Christ Jesus. God Almighty keep you all.
Executioner: My lord shall I put up your hair?
Capel: I, prythee do (lifting up his hands and eyes) O God, I do, with a perfect and willing heart, submit to thy will. O God, I do most willingly humble myself. (Kneeling down) I will try first how I can lye. (He lay his head on the block and addressed the executioner)
Capel: Am I well now?
Executioner: Yes
Capel: Here lie both my hands out, when I lift up my hand thus, (he lifted his right hand) you may strike.
He then made a short prayer, lifted his right hand, the executioner struck severing Capel's head with one blow. His servants placed his body in the waiting coffin, and it was transferred to the family seat, Hadham Hall in Essex. His body was then placed in the family vault in Little Hadham Church, Essex, and an outspoken inscription placed on the tomb stone which can still be seen.

> Here under lyeth interred the body of Arthur Capell Baron of Hadham who was murdered for his Loyalty to King Charles the First March 9th 1648 [1649] Here lyeth interred ye body of Elizabeth Lady Capell Wife of Arthur Lord Capell Onely daughter of Sr Charles Morrison Kt She departed this life ye 26th of Jan, 1660.

7. Tower Green

The location of the scaffold at Tower Green is not known exactly. Furthermore, only seven people are known to have been executed here. The victims were buried only a short distance away in St Peter ad Vincula, which lies directly behind the area of execution.

Chapel of St Peter ad Vincula where many of the victims of execution were interred. The railed area in the foreground is the official site of the scaffold.

The scaffold was built specially for each execution, and not always put precisely in the same place. Those executed here were William, Lord Hastings (June 1483), Anne Boleyn (19 May 1536), Margaret Pole, Countess of Salisbury (27 May, 1541), Katherine Howard (13 Feb 1542), and executed on the same day Jane, Viscountess Rochford. Lady Jane Grey (12 February 1554), and Robert Devereux, Earl of Essex (25 February 1601). The area inside the Tower was enclosed and protected against unruly crowds.

Anne Boleyn

Anne Boleyn (c. 1504–19 May 1536) was the daughter of the Earl of Wiltshire and she became the second wife of Henry VIII. The events leading to the scaffold are well known and the charges against her included adultery, incest and treason. It is possible through eyewitness accounts to reconstruct the events of her final day. Kingston, the Constable of the Tower, wrote to Thomas Cromwell, Henry's faithful servant:

> This morning she sent for me, that I might be with her at such time as she received the good Lord, to the intent I should hear her speak as touching her innocency alway to be clear. And in the writing of this she sent for me, and at my coming she said, 'Mr. Kingston, I hear I shall not die afore noon, and I am very sorry therefore, for I thought to be dead by this time and past my pain'. I told her it should be no pain, it was so little. And then she said, 'I heard say the executioner was very good, and I have a little neck,' and then put her hands about it, laughing heartily. I have seen many men and also women executed, and that they have been in great sorrow, and to my knowledge this lady has much joy in death. Sir, her almoner is continually with her, and had been since two o'clock after midnight.

Her nerve held even onto the scaffold:

> All these being on a scaffold made there for the execution, the said Queen Anne said as followeth: Masters, I here humbly submit me to the law, as the law hath judged me, and as for mine offences, God knoweth them, I remit them to God, beseeching him to have mercy on my soul; and I beseech Jesu save my Sovereign and master the

King, the most goodliest, and gentlest Prince that is, and long to reign over you, which words she spake with a smiling countenance: which done, she kneeled down on both her knees, and said, To Jesu Christ I commend my soul and with that word suddenly the hangman of Calais smote off her head at one stroke with a sword: her body with the head was buried in the choir of the Chapel in the Tower.

Margaret Pole

Margaret Pole, Countess of Salisbury (1473-1541) was the daughter of George Plantagenet and Isabella Neville. Her father was a brother to two kings, Edward IV and Richard III. Henry VIII without doubt felt that it would be too dangerous to allow her to live. She was arrested at the behest of Thomas Cromwell who introduced a Bill of Attainder against her in May 1539 for treason. She was immediately sent to the Tower where for two years she was kept under harsh conditions. In April 1541 there was an uprising in the north of England, and Henry, in his usual ruthless manner, believed it would be safer to remove a possible focus of discontent. On the morning of 27 May, she was told that she had an hour to prepare for her death. Her response was that she had not committed any crime. She was then taken to Tower Green where a low wooden block had been placed. There were 150 witnesses to the events that followed, and accounts of what happened vary. An account that originated with the main chronicler of the life of Henry VIII, Lord Herbert of Cherbury, is the one that is the most likely:

> ...She was the last lineal descendent of the Plantaganets; and, although past seventy years of age, possessed a masculine courage and spirit which was worthy of that race. On being designed to lay her neck on the block, she refused, declaring that it belonged to traitors to do so, and bidding the executioner take her life as he best could. Thus dared in the performance of his office, a horrid scene occurred; the countess moved swiftly round the scaffold, tossing her head from one side to the other, and avoiding

Margaret Pole, Countess of Salisbury.

the blows which were aimed at her; nor was the appalling spectacle concluded till her grey locks, which streamed over her shoulders, were covered with blood.

Catherine Howard

Catherine Howard was born in around 1520, the daughter of Lord Edmund Howard and Joyce Culpepper, and the niece of the Duke of Norfolk. She was also the first cousin of Anne Boleyn, Henry's second wife. She was poorly educated, and it is believed that her upbringing in the licentious atmosphere of the Duchess of Norfolk's circle led to a number of relationships. One of these was a romance with Henry Mannox, her music teacher, sometime around 1536, when Catherine was aged somewhere between twelve and sixteen. After marrying Henry, Catherine unwisely brought Mannox into her household. It is not known whether they resumed their relationship – both denied it when the matter was brought up at her trial, though she admitted to some physical contact with him. In 1538 Catherine had fallen for Francis Dereham, a young secretary. At the insistence of the Dowager Duchess of Norfolk this relationship was terminated in 1539. Both parties promised to marry each other at some later date. Her uncle, the Duke of Norfolk, found Catherine a position at court as a lady-in-waiting to Henry's then queen, Anne of Cleves. Henry quickly found himself attracted to the vivacious Catherine, whose standing was being increasingly promoted by the Howard family as a means of gaining political influence. Henry's marriage to Anne was annulled and Henry very soon showered Catherine with gifts, and it was rumoured that she was pregnant by him. Henry married her quickly, probably in the hope of fathering a son.

Henry was nearly fifty, and Catherine was around thirty years younger. It transpired that she was not pregnant, and found Henry physically repugnant. Foolishly, in the open and gossip-ridden atmosphere of the court, she embarked on a romance with one of

Catherine Howard.

Henry's courtiers, Thomas Culpepper. This relationship was encouraged and facilitated by one of Catherine's ladies-in-waiting, Lady Rochford. Catherine's activities, both before and after her marriage to Henry, were too well known to be kept secret and in the end, by late 1541, these rumours reached Thomas Cranmer, Archbishop of Canterbury, and an advisor to Henry. She was arrested on 12 November 1541. She was lodged in the Queen's Apartments, which still remain, overlooking Tower Green.

Contemporary accounts of the demise of Catherine Howard are scarce, the best known being that of the Spanish ambassador of the time, Eustace Chapuys:

> This year on 13 November Sir Thomas Wriothesley, secretary to the king, came to Hampton Court to the queen, and called all the ladies and gentlewomen and her servants into the great chamber, and there openly before them declared certain offenses she had committed in misusing her body with certain persons before the king's time, because of which he there discharged all her household; and the morning after she was taken to Sion, with my Lady Bainton and two other gentlewomen and certain of her servants to wait on her there until the king's further pleasure. And various people were taken to the Tower of London, such as my Lady Rochford, Master Culpepper, one of the king's privy chamber, and others.
>
> On 1 December Thomas Culpepper, one of the gentlemen of the king's privy chamber, and Francis Dorand, [Dereham] gentleman, were arraigned at the Guildhall in London, for high treason against the king's majesty, in misdemeanour with the queen, as appeared by their indictment which they confessed to, and they were sentenced to be drawn, hanged, and quartered, the lord mayor sitting there as chief, the lord chancellor on his right hand, and the Duke of Norfolk on his left hand, the Duke of Suffolk, the lord privy seal, the earls of Sussex, of Hertford, and various others of the king's council sitting with all the judges also in commission that day. And on 10 December the said Culpepper and Dorand were drawn from the Tower of London to Tyburn, and there Culpepper, after exhorting the people to pray for him, stood on the ground by the gallows, knelt down and had his head struck off; and then Dorand was hanged, dismembered, disembowelled, beheaded and quartered. Culpepper's body was buried at St Sepulchre's Church near Newgate, and their head were set on London Bridge.

Her demise came quickly when on the Sunday evening she was informed that she would die on the Monday. She requested the block be brought to her so that she could rehearse the final act of placing her head on it. Despite her fear she managed to undertake the ritual of the scaffold, giving a short, quiet speech in which she acknowledged the legitimacy of her punishment and prayed for Henry's preservation and God's forgiveness. She was interred in the Chapel of St Peter ad Vincula.

Lady Jane Grey, 1554

One of the earliest sources for the demise of Lady Jane Grey is a pocket diary covering the period from July 1553 to October 1554. In a foreword to the printed edition, dated 1850, we are told that 'it is written, or rather scribbled, in so bad a hand' and that 'it is the authority for the interesting account given by Stowe and Holinshed, of

Lady Jane Grey.

the execution of Lord Guilford Dudley and Lady Jane Grey, as well as for the greater part of their narrative of the progress of events whilst the council administered the government of the realm in the name of "Jane the Queene." In the *Harleian Catalogue* it is stated, that 'this book formerly belonged to Mr. John Stowe, who took from thence many passages which may be found in his Annals, at the reign of Queen Mary...'

When Henry VIII's son Edward VI was dying, the Dudley family attempted to disbar both daughters of Henry, Elizabeth and Mary, from taking the throne. The throne would be diverted in favour of Lady Jane Grey, daughter of the Duke of Suffolk, who had married Guilford Dudley. This was effectively a coup that failed, and the price paid, by both Jane and Guilford, high.

> Guilforde Ddley, sone to the late duke of Northumberland, husbande to the lady Jane Grey, daughter of the duke of Suffolke, who at his going out took by the hands Sir Anthony Browne, maister John Throgmorton, and many other gentyllmen, praying them to praie for him; and without the bullwarke [Sir Thomas]Offeley the sheryve received him and brought him to the scaffold, where, after a small declaration, having no gostlye father [a priest] with him, he kneeled downe and said his praiers; then holding up his eyes and hands to God many tymes; and at last, after he had desired the people to pray for him, he laide himself along, and his hedd upon the block, which was at one stroke of the axe taken from him.

The account continues:

> Note, the lorde marques [Marquess of Northampton] stode upon the Devyl's towre, and saw the execution. His [Guildford's] carcase thrown into a carre, and his hed in a cloth, he was brought into the chapell within the Tower, wher the lady Jane, whose lodging was in Partrige's house, dyd see his ded carcase taken out of the cart, aswell as she dyd see him before on live on going to his deathe – a sight to hir no lesse than death.

> By this tyme was ther a scaffolde made upon the grene over agaynst the White tower, for the saide lady Jane to die apon ... Who with hir husband was appynted to have ben put to deathe the fryday before, but was staied tyll then, for what cause is not knowen, unless yt were because hir father was not then come into the Tower. The saide lady, being nothing abashed neither with feare of her owne deathe, which then approached, neither with the sight of the ded carcasse of hir husbande, when he was brought in to the chappell, cause fourthe, the levetenannt leding hir, in the same gown wherin she was arrayned, hir countenance nothing abashed, neither her eyes anything moysted with teares, although her ij.gentylwomen, mistress Elizabeth Tylney and mistress Eleyn, wonderfully wept, with a boke in her hande, wheron she praied all the way till she came to the saide scaffold wheron when she was mounted...

The manuscript unfortunately breaks off mid-sentence. The 1850 editor then comments that the diary narrative so far is that which is adopted by both Stowe and Holinshed, but at this point Holinshed perhaps embellishes the account with the addition of the words,

> Wereon when she mounted, this noble young ladie, as she was indued with singular gifts both of learning and knowledge, so was she as patient and milde as any lambe at hir execution, and a little before her death uttered these words...

Such embellishments act as a warning against trusting early verbatim accounts of historic events. The manuscript then continues with a subheading which reads, 'The Ende of the lady Jane Dudley, [Grey] daughter of the duke of Suffolk, upon the scaffold, at the houre of her death.'

> First, when she mounted upon the scaffold, she sayd to the people standing thereabout: 'Good people, I am come hether to die, and by a lawe I am condemned to the same. The facte, in dede, against the quenes highnesse was unlawfull, and the consenting thereunto by me: but touching the procurement and desyre therof by me or on my halfe, I doo wash my handes therof in innocencie, before God, and the face of you, good Christian people, this day,' ... and therewith she wrong her handes, in which she had hir booke. Then she sayd, 'I pray you all, good Christan people, to beare me witnesse that I dye a true Christian woman, and that I looke to be saved by none other meane, but only by the mercy of God in the merites of the blood of his only sonne Jesus Christ: and I confesse, when I dyd know the word of God I neglected the same, loved my selfe and the world, and therefore this plague or punyshmment is happily and worthily happened unto me for my sins; and yet I thank God of his goodnesse that he hath thus geven me a tyme and respet to repent. And now, good people, while I am alive, I pray you to assist me with your prayers.' And then knelyng down, she turned to Feckenham, [the dean of St Paul's] saying, 'Shall I say this psalme?' And he said, 'Yea.' Then she said the psalme of *Miserere mei Deus*, in English, in most devout manner, to the end. Then she stode up and gave her maiden mistris Tilney her gloves and handkercher, and her book to maister Bruges, the lyvetenantes brother; forthwith she untyed her gown. The hangman went to her to help her therewith; then she desyred him to let her alone, and

turning towards her two gentlewomen, who helped her off therwith, and also with her frose past and neckercher, geving to her a fayre handkercher to knytte about her eyes. Then the hangman kneeled downe, and asked her forgevenesse, whome she forgave most willingly. Then he willed her to stand upon the strawe: which doing, she sawe the block. Then she sayd, 'I pray you dispatch me quickly.' Then she kneeled down, saying, 'Wil you take it of before I lay me downe?' and the hangman answered her, 'No, madame.' She tyed the kercher about her eys; then feeling for the blocke, saide, 'What shall I do? Where is it?' One of the standers-by guyding her therunto, she layde her heade down upon the block, and stretched forth her body and said: 'Lord, into thy hands I commende my spirite!' And so she ended.

Robert Devereux, Earl of Essex

Devereux (1567–1601) was a favourite of Elizabeth I, but fell into disfavour over his handling of affairs in Ireland and was further disgraced when he led a rebellion in

Robert Devereux, 2nd Earl of Essex, 1596 (1566–1601).

Victorians observe the execution site within the Tower area.

London intended to confront the queen. On 19 February 1601 Essex was tried and found guilty of treason. It is possible that on being condemned to death he believed the queen would pardon him. At the height of their passion Elizabeth had given him a ring with the promise that whatever he should commit, if he were to send her the ring she would forgive him. After being condemned it is believed that he gave the ring to his relative Admiral Howard's wife, but her husband, a bitter enemy of Essex, on hearing that she had the ring, forbade that the ring be passed to the queen. It is said that Elizabeth believed that Essex had chosen to die out of haughtiness and pride rather than plead for mercy but even so, when it came to signing the death warrant she vacillated. A while later, after the execution when the Admiral's wife was dying, she called Elizabeth to her bedside and confessed that her husband had held the ring back. Elizabeth was overcome with grief and died soon after.

The earl was extremely popular and it was felt that it would be too dangerous to execute him on Tower Hill. Tower Green was thus chosen. He was being held in the Tower so he could be executed and interred with the minimum of public attention. He was escorted to the scaffold by the lieutenant of the Tower and sixteen guards at 8 a.m. on 25 February 1601. A small seating area was built close to the scaffold for a number of lords to observe the proceedings. Essex was dressed in 'a gowne of wrought velvet, a blacke satin suite, a felt hat blacke, a little ruffe about his necke'. With him were also three clergymen or 'divines'. He gave a short speech or confession. He then removed his doublet to reveal a scarlet waistcoat. Then 'lying flat along on the bordes, and laying downe his head and fitting it upon the blocke, his head was severed from his bodie by the axe at three stroaks, but the first deadly and absolutely depryving all sence and motion'. Such was the popularity of Essex, that the executioner required the protection of the Sherriff of London to protect him 'from such as would have murthered him'. He was buried under the supervision of the Earl of Arundel and Duke of Norfolk in St Peters ad Vincula.

8. Tower Hill

Location of Scaffold

Executions of those not noble enough or deserving of privacy took place outside of the Tower enclosure, slightly to the north-west on Tower Hill. The author of *Old and New London*, 1878, in attempting to discover the exact place, decided that it altered over the centuries but was a locality in its own right.

> Hatton, in 1708 (Queen Anne) mentions Tower Hill as 'a spacious place extending round the west and north parts of the Tower, where there are many good new

The official site of the scaffold at Tower Hill.

Inset: Memorial plaque on Tower Hill.

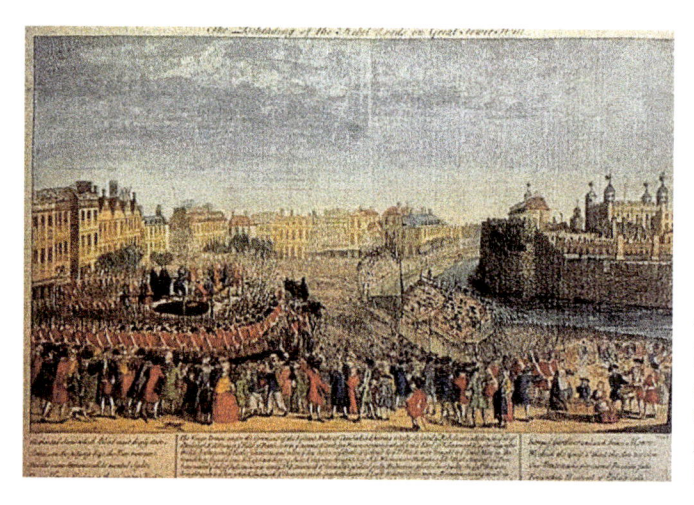

'The Beheading of the Rebel Lords on Great Tower Hill', c. 1746. The execution of the leaders of the Jacobite rebels captured after the Battle of Culloden.

A similar view over 250 years later to that of 'The Beheading of the Rebel Lords.'

buildings, mostly inhabited by gentry and merchants'. The tide of fashion and wealth had not yet set in strongly westward. An old plan of the Tower in 1563 shows us the posts of the scaffold for state criminals, a good deal north of Tower Street and a little northward of Legge Mount, the great north-west corner of the Tower fortifications. In the reign of Edward IV, the scaffold was erected at the charge of the king's officers, and many controversies arose at various times, about the respective boundaries, between the City and the Lieutenant of the Tower.

James Scott, Duke of Monmouth and Buccleuch

Monmouth (1649–85) was a son of Charles II by his mistress Lucy Walter. He had no claim to the throne on the death of his father, though he always alleged that Charles had secretly married his mother. However, the unpopularity of James II, a Catholic brother of Charles, persuaded him to lead a rebellion in 1685, around six months after the accession of James. It was put down at the Battle of Sedgemoor, near Bridgewater, on 6 July and the event is chiefly remembered for the brutality of the notorious Judge Jeffreys, who sentenced 320 persons to death, and 800 to transportation in a series of trials that had little to do with justice.

Roberts, in his massive two-volume work on Monmouth, claims to draw his report of the demise of the Duke on Tower Hill from a 'very scarce sheet of four folio pages, printed at the time by authority'. He wrote,

> An Account of what passed at the Execution of the late Duke of Monmouth, on Wednesday the 15th of July, 1685, on Tower Hill; together with a paper signed by himself that Morning in the Tower, in the Presence of the Lords Bishops of Ely and Bath and Wells, Dr. Tennison, and Dr. Hooper.

Roberts notes that 'the lieutenant brought him [Monmouth] some steps without the fortress in his coach, and then delivered him to the sheriffs of the city, who conducted him on foot through a hedge of soldiery, accompanied by three officers with pistols

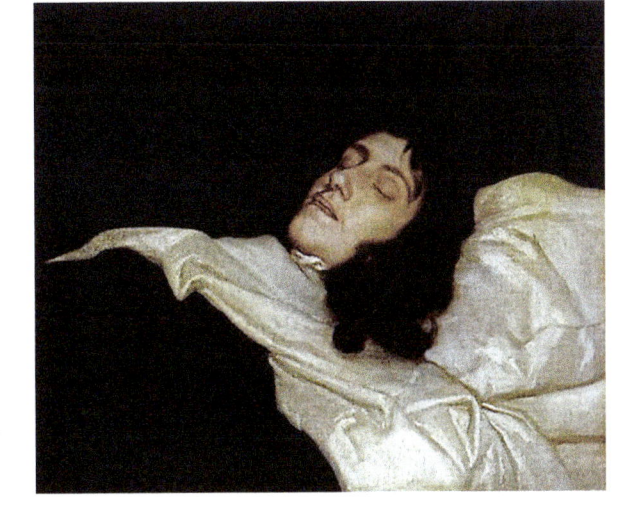

James Scott, Duke of Monmouth and Buccleuch (1649–85), Son of Charles II, by Lucy Walter. It is reported that it took eight blows of the axe to despatch Monmouth. A picture painted after his death with his head sewn back on.

in their hands, and who ascended the scaffold with him, and remained near him till the execution'. Another source referred to by Roberts says that 'on Monmouth's first appearance a murmur of sighs and groans went round the whole assembly, which by degrees sank into a breathless silence, as if every syllable he had to utter was sacred, and not to be profaned with the unhallowed mixture of any vulgar sound'. James II made a concession to his nephew by allowing the scaffold to be draped in black for mourning, and allowing his body to be given to friends to be 'disposed of as they shall think fit'. The following description of the execution seems authentic as opposed to many politically motivated reports. Some non-relevant sections have been removed.

> The late Duke of Monmouth came from the Tower to the Scaffold, [at Ten, A.M., Wednesday, 15th July, attended by the Bishop of Ely, the Bishop of Bath and Wells, Dr. Tennison, and Dr. Hooper, which four the King was graciously pleased to send him, as his Assistants, to prepare him for Death; and the late Duke himself entreated all four of them to accompany him to the Place of Execution, and to continue with him to the last. The two Bishops, going in the Lieutenant's Coach with him to the Bars, made seasonable and devout Applications to him all the way; and one of them desired him not to be surprised if they, to the very last, upon the Scaffold, renewed those Exhortations to a Particular Repentance, which they had so often repeated before. At his first coming upon the Scaffold he looked for the Executioner, and seeing him, said, 'Is this the man to do the business? Do your work well...' Then the late Duke of Monmouth began to speak, [to] someone or other of the Assistants, during the whole time, applying themselves to him. There then followed a long battle of words between Monmouth and those appointed to attend him. They repeatedly urged him to confess and repent his rebellion, which he declined to do and referred them to a paper he had written on the matter.

Monmouth. I shall say but very little, I come to die, I die a Protestant of the Church of England.
Assistant. My Lord, if you be of the Church of England, you must acknowledge the Doctrine of Non-resistance to be true?
Monmouth. If I acknowledge the Doctrine of the Church of England in general, that includes all.
Monmouth then raised the matter of his relationship with Lady Henrietta Wentworth.
Assistant. In your Opinion, perhaps, Sir, as you have been told [i.e. in the Tower] but this is not fit Discourse in this Place.
Mr Sheriff Goslin. Sir, I hoped to have head of your Repentance for the Treason and Bloodshed which have been committed.
Monmouth. I dy very penitent.
Assistant. My Lord. It is fit to be Particular, and, considering the Publick Evil you have done, you ought to do as much good now as possibly you can, by a Publick acknowledgement.
Monmouth. What I have thought fit to say of Publick affairs is in a Paper which I have signed. I refer to my paper.

And later:

Monmouth. I repent of all things that a true Christian ought to repent of. I am to die. Pray, Mr. Lord.
Assistant. Then (My Lord) we can only recommend you to the Mercy of God; but we cannot pray with that Chearfulness and Encouragement as we should if you had made a Particular Acknowledgement.

And then again:

Monmouth. I am sorry for invading the Kingdom and for the Blood that has been shed; and for the Souls which may have been lost by my means. I am sorry it ever happened [which he spake softly].
Mr Sheriff Vandeput [to some that stood at a distance.] He says he is very sorry for invading the Kingdom. .
Assistant. God Almighty of his infinite Mercy forgive you. Here are great numbers of spectators; here are the Sheriff's; they represent the Great City; and in speaking to them, you speak to a whole City: make some Satisfaction by owning your Crime before them.

He was silent here. Then all went to solemn Commendatory Prayers, which continued for a good space, the late Duke of Monmouth and the company kneeling, and joining in them with great fervency. Prayers being ended, before he, and the four who assisted him, were risen from their knees, he was again earnestly exhorted to a true and thorough repentance. After they were risen up, he was exhorted to pray for the king, and was asked whether he did not desire to send some dutiful message to his majesty, and to recommend his wife and children to his majesty's favour.

Monmouth. What harm have they done? Do it, if you please; I pray for him and for all men.
Monmouth. [After some pause, he answered] Amen.
Then he spake to the executioner, concerning his undressing, &c., and he would have no cap, &c., and at the beginning of his undressing, it was said to him on this manner: -
Assistant. My Lord, you have been bred a Souldier: you will do a generous Christian thing, if you please to go to the Bail, and speak to the Souldiers, and say that here you stand, a sad example of Rebellion, and entreat them and the People to be Loyal and Obedient to the King.
Monmouth. I have said I will make no Speeches – I will make no Speeches – I come to die.
Assistant. My Lord, ten words will be enough.
Monmouth. [Then calling his Servant, and giving him something like a Toothpick-Case] Here [said he], give this to the Person to whom you are to deliver the other things.
Monmouth. [To the executioner] Here are six guineas for you: pray do your business well; do not serve me as you did my Lord Russell. I have heard you struck him three or four times. Here [to his servant], take these remaining guineas, and give them to him, if he does his work well.

Executioner. I hope I shall.
Monmouth. If you strike me twice, I cannot promise you not to stir.
Monmouth lay down and then rose up again and asked to see the axe. He felt it and said 'I fear it is not sharp enough'.
Executioner. It is sharp enough and heavy enough.

Then he lay down again.

It is probably understandable that the authorities do not refer to one of the worst decapitations undertaken at Tower Hill. It has been commented that the executioner's nerves on the scaffold were so bad, that he 'was much more agitated than he who was to suffer'.

The contemporary German pamphlet provides a sickening account of the remaining events of 15 July 1685:

…the botcherly dog, the executioner, did so barbarously act his pairt, that he could not at fyve stroaks of the ax sever the head from the body. At the first, which made only a slight dash in his neck, his [Monmouth's]body heaved up and his head turned about; the second stroke made only a deeper dash, after which the body moved; the third not doing the work, he threw away the axe, and said 'God damme, I can doe no more, my heart fails me.' The executioner declared that his limbs were stiffened (probably paralysed with fear) and that he would willingly give forty guineas to anyone who would finish the work. The bystanders had much ado to forbear throwing him over the scaffold; but made him take the axe again, threatening to kill him if he did not do his duty better. With two strokes more, not being able to finish the work, he was fain to draw forth his long knife, and with it to cut off the remaining part of his neck. He could not hold the head: he only showed it once to the people. If there had been no guard before the soldiers, to conduct the executioner away, the people would have torn him to pieces, so great was their indignation at the barbarous usage of the late Duke of Monmouth at his hands. After his death, the people ran in crowds to the scaffold, and dipped, some their handkerchiefs and some their shirts, in his blood, as it is the custom to do on such occasions, notwithstanding the danger from the thrusts of the halberts and pikes, which they carried away as a precious relic.

Immediately after his death Monmouth's head was re-attached to the body, in order to allow a portrait to be drawn. (*See illustration*). He was placed in a black velvet covered coffin which stood waiting on the scaffold and driven to St Peters ad Vincula at the Tower in a six horse mourning coach. The body was then interred under the communion table of the chapel.

Executions of William Boyd, 4th Earl of Kilmarnock and Lord Balmerino

The trial of William Boyd, 4th earl of Kilmarnock, for high treason in 1746 was remarkable for the semblance of fairness offered to the Scottish peers. He and a number of other Scottish nobles, who were part of the Jacobite Rebellion, were captured after the Battle of Culloden in April 1746 and brought to London for trial.

Plaque on the site of the Tower Hill Scaffold.

The execution itself on Tower Hill was unusual in that a scaffold was erected adjoining No. 14 Tower Hill, against a house in which the earl, and his fellow peer in misfortune, Lord Balmerino, waited until everything was ready. The two men walked from the Tower, where they were both being held, and in the house prepared for their executions in an almost leisurely and relaxed manner. The executions reflect the protocols and etiquette of the scaffold of the time – much of the show and behaviour of the 'age of politeness'. On being informed of his execution, to take place the following Monday, 'Lord Kilmarnock received this news with the outward behaviour of a man, that knew and felt the importance of the scene of death, but without any marks of disorder, without any unbecoming anxiousness or terror.' The Sheriff, who brought the news to the earl, out of sympathy for him, warned him of the nature of the ordeal he was about to undergo in order to allow him to prepare himself:

> …I told him, that all mankind were really under sentence of death, though they knew not the manner or precise time when it would be executed; it might be to anyone as soon or sooner than his own; that they not expecting it, nor having such timely and certain notice of it, might die wholly unguarded and unprepared; while he had warning, and the most awakening motives to fit himself in the best manner possible for this grand and decisive event.

The earl answered that he was a good Christian and had, as such, no fear concerning death; indeed 'he thought it a trifle' and with regards the mechanism of his death he had 'no great reason to be terrified, for the stroke [of the axe] appeared to be scarce so much as the pain of drawing a tooth or the first shock of the cold bath upon a weak and fearful temper'. The sheriff, Williamson, obviously had empathy and respect for the earl and engaged in some gentle psychotherapy to prepare Kilmarnock for what awaited him. He did not want Kilmarnock to show any involuntary shock.

William Boyd, 4th Earl of Kilmarnock (1704–46).

The under-sheriff noted that Williamson, on the Saturday preceding the execution, 'gave him a minute detail of all the circumstances of solemnity and outward terror that would accompany it, and that he 'heard it with ... much shew of composure':

> He was told that on Monday, about ten in the morning, the sheriffs would come to demand the prisoners, who would be delivered them at the gate of the Tower; that from thence, if their lordships thought proper, they should walk on foot to the house appointed on Tower-hill for their reception, where the rooms would be hung with black, to make the more decent and solemn appearance, and that the scaffold also would be covered with black cloth; that his lordship might repose and prepare himself, in the room fitted up for him, as long as he thought it convenient, remembering only, that the warrant for the execution was limited to, and consequently expired at one o' clock; that because of a complaint made by the lord Kenmure, that the block was too low, it was ordered to be raised to the height of two feet; that it might be the more firmly fixed, props would be placed directly under it, that the certainty or decency of the execution might not be obstructed by any concussion, or sudden jerk of the body. All this lord Kilmarnock, without the least visible emotion, expressed his satisfaction in: but when the general told him, that two mourning hearses would be provided, and placed close by the scaffold, that when the head was struck off, the coffins might soon be taken out to receive the bodies; he said that he thought it would be better for the coffin to be upon the scaffold, for by that means the bodies would be still sooner removed out of sight.

Once on the scaffold, Kilmarnock embraced his friends, and took his leave of them. He was then 'introduced' to the executioner who asked his forgiveness for the 'painful task allotted to him'.

Horace Walpole comments that the executioner was dressed in white with a white apron and out of 'tenderness' concealed the axe behind him. One account says that when Kilmarnock 'beheld the fatal scaffold covered with black cloth; the executioner with his axe and his assistants; the saw-dust, which was soon to be drenched with his blood; the coffin prepared to receive the limbs which were yet warm with life; above all, the immense display of human countenances which surrounded the scaffold like a sea, all eyes being bent on the sad object of the preparation, his natural feelings broke forth in a whisper to the friend on whose arm he leaned, "Home, this is terrible!" He then handed the executioner a purse containing payment, and gave him final instructions: he was to wait for the signal which would be when he dropped his handkerchief. Kilmarnock's servants then helped him to take his coat off, and place his hair under a cap, 'lest the blow be intercepted' after which, with total composure he knelt down at the block and proceeded to pray for about six minutes. He then dropped the handkerchief, on which the headsman struck, decapitating him with one blow. The head was placed in a piece of scarlet baize and placed in the waiting coffin along with his body. It was then handed over to friends. Horace Walpole's account says that when Kilmarnock came to the scaffold although he was resolute he was also 'much terrified'. When the earl, after 'testing' the block several times, knelt down at the block he showed a 'visible unwillingness to depart', taking five minutes to drop the handkerchief, which was his signal to the executioner to strike.

With the death of his friend, Lord Kilmarnock, it was now the turn of Lord Balmerino. The under-sheriff went to the house. As he entered Balmerino said to him 'I suppose my lord Kilmarnock is no more?' He then asked how well the executioner had performed, and on being told, said 'then it was well; and now, gentlemen I will detain you no longer for I desire not to protract my life'. An eyewitness reports that,

> His lordship then observing the executioner with the axe in his hand, took it from him, and having felt the edge, returned it him again, at the same time shewing him where to strike the blow, and animating him to do it with resolution; 'For in that, friend, (said his lordship) will consist your mercy.'

Unfortunately for Balmerino the executioner took two blows of the axe:

> ...the executioner was so terrified at his lordship's intrepidity, and the suddenness of the signal, that notwithstanding he struck his lordship in the part directed, yet the force of the blow was not sufficient to sever the head from the body, though (happily) sufficient to deprive him of all sensation.

The observer continues to describe in detail what then happened:

> ...After the first blow, his lordship's head fell back upon his shoulders, but being afterward severed at two more gentle blows, was then received into a piece of red baize, and with his body deposited in his coffin, and delivered to his friends.

The Chambers' *Book of Days* (1869) notes that the house

> still exists, marked as No. 14 Tower Hill. The two lords were in succession led out of this house on to the scaffold, Kilmarnock suffering before Balmerino, in melancholy reference to his higher rank in the peerage. Their mutilated bodies, after being deposited in their respective coffins, are said to have been brought back into the house, and in proof of this, a trail of blood is still visible along the hall and up the first flight of stairs. There is a contemporary print of the execution, representing the scaffold as surrounded by a wide square of dragoons, beyond which are great multitudes of people, many of them seated in wooden galleries. The decapitated lords were all respectfully buried in St. Peter's Chapel within the Tower.

Simon Fraser, 11th Lord Lovat

Lovat (*c*. 1667–9 April 1747) was a colourful character who led a turbulent life. Having supported the Hanoverian succession, in 1745 he changed his mind and backed the Stuarts. He was present at Culloden, and after the subsequent rout he fled. He was found hiding inside a hollow tree and brought to London for trial for high treason. He conducted himself at his trial in 1747 with a certain levity, which was noted by a number of contemporary sources who felt that Lovat was not taking his impending fate with any seriousness.

Simon Fraser, 11th Baron Lovat, in 1746 – the last person to be beheaded on Tower Hill.

The execution block that was used at, and probably made for, the execution of Lord Lovat on display in the Tower.

Inset: Detail of the block. Clearly visible on the top of the block are the grooves where the axe fell.

The conduct of Lovat at his trial and execution was most extraordinary. When a principal witness had given in his testimony upon which depended the issue of the trial, the defendant being asked if he had any question to propose to the witness, replied, 'I only wish him joy of his young wife' and after sentence of death had been pronounced against him – in the horrible terms in which sentences for treason are delivered – as he was retiring, he called out, 'Fare you well, my lords: we shall not all meet again in one place.' At the execution, however, he indulged in no offensive levity, but behaved with great propriety, calling out just at last, '*Dulce et decorum est pro patria mori*.' It is glorious to die for one's country.

State Trials and Proceedings offers the reader 'an account of the behaviour of Simon Lord Lovat, from the time his death-warrant was delivered, to the day of his execution. By a Gentleman who attended his Lordship in his last moments'. Lovat was well aware that his behaviour prior to execution would be the subject of scrutiny, and wanted to leave a good impression. *State Trials and Proceedings* tells us that on the Friday 3rd April, six days prior to his execution, when the messenger bearing the warrant for his execution arrived, Lovat 'thanked him kindly for the favour ... and assured him he was well satisfied with his doom'. On that same day, he is described as smoking his pipe and being 'very cheerful'. He refers to his portliness – as depicted in his caricature by Hogarth – as causing problems for the executioner. In fact a special 'engine' was being constructed to take account of the problem. He said that 'as his neck was very short, the executioner would be puzzled to find it out with his axe; and if such a machine was made, they might call it Lord Lovat's Maiden'. We are also told that contrary to popular belief, Lovat was not a drunkard as he 'never drank more than two pints of wine a day ... and never any without water'. On the Thursday of his execution,

> ...his lordship awaked about three o'clock in the morning, and prayed most devoutly. At five he got up, called for a glass of wine and water, according to his usual custom, and seemed still as cheerful as ever; then being placed in his chair, sat and read until seven, when he called for another glass of wine and water. About eight o'clock he desired Mr.Sherrington, one of the warders, to send his wig so that the barber might have time to comb it out. He then called for a purse to put his money in for the executioner, and desired it might be a good one, lest the gentleman should refuse it. Mr.Southbey, one of his lordship's warders, I remember, brought him two purses, the one a green silk knit, and the other a yellow canvass, but which his lordship made choice of I really forget; however, it was a purse, as he observed, that no man would dislike with ten guineas in it ... As his lordship was now within a few hours of death and had behaved with such surprising intrepidity during his whole confinement, I was the more particular in observing every little incident that happened. But though he had a great share of memory and understanding ... His behaviour was all of a piece, and he was the same facetious companion now, as he was before sentence was passed against him...

In a parody which borders on studied nonchalance, again probably with an eye to future chroniclers, he commented that his barber had brought his wig and had not powdered it on account of it being a rainy day. His attending companion reports, 'He seemed angry, and said, "That he went to the block with pleasure, and he had a suit of velvet embroidered, he would wear it on that occasion".' In conversation with his barber, he commented that he would be in heaven by one o' clock, which was his reason for being so happy. Impending doom did little to constrain his Lordship's appetite. At 9.30, a couple of hours before his execution, 'his lordship called for a plate of minced veal, eat [en] very heartily ... he then called for some wine and water, and drank the health of several of his friends'. It was then, at 10 a.m. while Lovat was taking his final drinks in the Tower, that with the crowds gathering on Tower Hill in large numbers the grandstand collapsed: 'At ten a terrible accident happened upon the hill, by the fall of a scaffold, which put all the people in great confusion; several persons were killed, and numbers maimed and bruised.' It was shortly after this incident that the sheriffs of London called for Lovat, who asked for a short time to pray, and then said that he was ready. As an ill, corpulent eighty-year-old man, he proceeded very slowly down the stairs in the Tower maintaining an air of politeness, but complaining that the stairs were 'very troublesome to him'.

> When he came to the door, he bowed to the people, and he was then put into the governor's coach, and carried to the outer gate where he was taken out of the governor's coach, and delivered to the sheriffs of the city of London and county of Middlesex, who conducted him in another coach to a house near the scaffold which had been lined in black cloth for his lordship's reception…

The civilised, social manner of the process of execution is emphasised when Lovat requested of the sheriffs that he might have the favour of being attended by his friends and relatives. This was agreed and they were allowed into the house. Lovat, in return for this favour, informed the sheriffs that 'it was a considerable consolation to him that his body fell into the hands of gentlemen of so much honour' and he then added, as if to dispel any concerns of that nature that, 'I will give you, gentlemen, and the government no farther trouble, for I shall make no speech; though I have a paper to leave, with which you may do as you think proper.' Lovat then said further prayers after which the sheriff asked him 'if he would refresh himself with a glass of wine?' Lovat replied that he would take some 'burnt brandy and bitters'. Lovat, as if attending a genteel social occasion, then turned to the sheriff during which a civilised conversation of a practical nature took place and he informed the sheriff that 'he was ready to go whenever he pleased', to which the sheriff replied,

> 'My Lord … I would not hurry your lordship', and taking out his watch, said, 'There is half an hour good, if your lordship don't tarry too long upon the scaffold.' Lovat then desired that his clothes might be delivered to his friends with his corpse, and not given to the executioner, and said, 'For that reason he should give him [the executioner] ten guineas.' He then asked, if he might have the axe brought him to feel if it was sharp, and desired that his head, when taken off, might be received in a cloth, and put into the coffin.

The sheriff, ever mindful of the original sentence that Lovat should have been hanged, drawn, and quartered, conferred with some 'gentlemen present' and commented that he had

> received a warrant in the usual form for the execution of his lordship, and as it had not been customary of late years to expose the head at the four corners of the scaffold, he really thought he might indulge his lordship with a promise as to that point, for he did not think he could expose the head (though it was desired, and indeed ordered by a message) without being liable to censure; adding withal, 'That he was truly sensible of the duty he owed his majesty, and should always pay a great regard to the orders he received from his grace the Duke of Newcastle, or any of his

ministry.' And then turning to his lordship, told him, 'That what he desired should be punctually observed.'

With the assistance of two gentlemen, Lovat then proceeded to the scaffold. Going up the steps he looked around him and said, 'God save us! Why should there be such a bustle about taking off an old grey head that cannot get up three steps without two men to support it?' In contrast to the rough-and-tumble mob of Tyburn, a much more civilised protocol unfolded on Tower Hill. The same gentleman who had accompanied Lovat from the time of his condemnation reports,

> The first person he sought when he came upon the scaffold was the executioner, who was immediately presented to him; and after he had made his obeisance, my lord put his hand into his pocket, and pulled out a purse with ten guineas, saying, 'Here, Sir, is ten guineas for you, pray do your work well; for if you should cut and hack my shoulders, and I should be able to rise again, I shall be very angry with you.' He then sat down again, and repeated the following line out of Horace:
> '*Dulce et decorum est pro Patria mori.*'
> (Tis a glorious sad pleasant thing to die for our country.)
> He called for Mr. William Fraser, his solicitor and agent in Scotland, and holding up his gold-headed cane, said, 'I deliver you this cane in token of my sense of your faithful services, and of my committing to you all the power I have upon earth.' and he then took off his wig, ordered his cap to be put on, and having unloosed his cravat and the neck of his shirt, he kneeled down to the block, took hold of the cloth which was placed to receive his head, and pulled it close to him: but being placed too near the block, the executioner desired his lordship would remove a little farther back, which he did; and having placed his neck in a proper manner, he told the executioner that he would say a short prayer, and then drop his handkerchief as a signal. In this posture he remained about half a minute, and threw his handkerchief upon the floor, when the executioner at one blow severed his head from the body, which being received in a scarlet cloth, was wrapped up, and together with his body, put into the coffin, and carried in a hearse back to the Tower, where it remained till four o'clock, and was then taken away by an undertaker.

9. Lincoln's Inn Fields

It is difficult to imagine on a sunny spring day when the square is packed with suited men and women enjoying pleasant aspect of Lincoln's Inn for lunch and a peaceful break, that this was once a place of execution.

William, Lord Russell, executed at Lincoln Inn Fields, 1688.

William, Lord Russell

In the vicinity of the bandstand, on 21 July 1683, of Lord Russell (1639–83), a son of the 5th earl, later first Duke of Bedford, was executed after being implicated in the Rye House Plot, which planned to assassinate both Charles II and his brother, the future James II, on their way back from Newmarket – Rye House, owned by a Republican, was in Hoddesdon. An early suggestion was that Russell be executed in Southampton House, facing what is now Bloomsbury Square, but the king thought this indecent, and nearby Lincoln's Inn Fields was decided on. On his way to execution, as his carriage turned into Little Queen Street, just off what became part of Kingsway in the vicinity of Lincoln's Inn, he shed a tear 'at the remembrance of his wife'. Burnett wrote,

> Tillotson and I went with him in the coach to the place of execution. Some of the crowd that filled the streets wept, while others insulted. He was touched by the tenderness that the one gave him, but did not seem at all provoked by the other. He was singing psalms a great part of the way, and said he hoped to sing better soon. As he observed the great crowds of people all the way he said to us, 'I hope I shall quickly see a much better assembly.' When he came to the scaffold he walked about it four or five times. Then he turned to the sheriffs and delivered his paper. He protested that he had always been far from any designs on the King's life or government. He prayed God would preserve both, and the Protestant religion. He wished all Protestants might love one another, and not make way for Popery by their animosities. The substance of the paper he delivered to the sheriffs was, first, a profession of his religion and his sincerity in it; that he was of the Church of England, but wished all would unite together against the common enemy; that churchmen would be less severe, and Dissenters less scrupulous. He owned he had a great zeal against Popery, which he looked on as an idolatrous and bloody religion, but that, although he was at all times ready to venture his life for his religion or his country, yet this would never have carried him to any black or wicked design. No man had the impudence to move to him anything with relation to the king's life. He prayed heartily for him, that in

his person and government he might be happy, both in this world and the next. He protested that in the prosecution of the popish plot he had gone on in the sincerity of his heart, and that he never knew of any practice with the witnesses. He owned he had been earnest in the matter of the exclusion, as they best way in his opinion to secure both the king's life and the Protestant religion; and to that he imputed his present sufferings; but he forgave all concerned in them, and charged his friends to think of no revenge. He thought his sentence was hard, upon which he gave an account of all that had passed at Shepherd's. From the heats that were in choosing the sheriffs, he concluded that matter would end as it now did, and he was not much surprised to find it fall upon himself. He wished it might end in him: killing by law was the worst form of murder. He concluded with some very devout ejaculations. After he had delivered this paper, he prayed by himself; then Tillotson prayed with him. After that, he prayed again by himself, and then undressed himself, and laid his head on the block, without the least change of countenance; and it was cut off at two strokes.

What Burnet omitted to mention to the king was that the executioner, Jack Ketch, made such a poor job of the decapitation that four axe blows were required. After the first stroke, Russell looked up and said to the executioner 'You dog, did I give you 10 guineas to use me so inhumanely?' Five years later when the Duke of Monmouth

The plaque marking the execution place of William, Lord Russell, used to be near the bandstand in Lincolns Inn Fields.

St Michael's Church, Chenies, Bucks – the burial place of Lord William Russell.

The chapel belonging to the Dukes of Bedford.

mounted the scaffold at Tower Hill, and realised he had the same executioner as had executed Russell, he asked Ketch if he thought the axe was sharp enough, handed him 6 guineas, and promised him a further sum if he did his work properly, commenting, 'Pray do not serve me as you did my Lord Russell. I have heard you struck him four or five times; if you strike me twice, I cannot promise you not to stir.'

An inscription that read, 'On this spot was beheaded William, Lord Russell, a lover of constitutional liberty 21st July A.D. 1683' was once at the place of execution. The plaque is no longer there, but it was in the vicinity of the bandstand. Russell's body lies in the Bedford family chapel in St Michael's Church, Chenies, in Buckinghamshire near Amersham.

10. St Paul's Churchyard

The Gunpowder Plot Conspirators
The area around St Pauls Cathedral was an occasional site of execution, playing host to a series of well-known victims, namely those of four members of the Gunpowder Plot of 5 November 1605. During the reign of Edward II it had a reputation as a place where murders and robberies were committed, 'but the citizens then claimed the east part of the churchyard to be the place of assembly'.

Old St Paul's Cathedral prior to its destruction by the Great Fire in 1666.

The Executions

The Gunpowder Plot was discovered on 5 November 1605 and the conspirators were executed, some here at St Paul's, some at Westminster, in the following January.

In the contemporary news sheet, the *Weekely Newes*, the accused are referred to as 'the eight papists ... monsters in nature.' Of the offence itself the *Weekely Newes* describes it apoplectically as 'so odious in the ears of all human creatures that it could hardly be believed that so many monsters in nature should carry the shapes of men – murder!' The plotters were held at the Tower and tried at Westminster. The four to die at St Pauls were Everard Digby, the elder Winter, Grant and Bates. Following sentence they were taken back to the Tower and on 27 January 1606 were 'drawn upon sledges and hurdles into Saint Paul's Churchyard' the scaffold having been 'made on purpose for their execution'. The *Weekely Newes* reports,

> First went up Digby, a man of goodly personage and a manly aspect, but with a vain and superstitious crossing of himself he betook himself to his Latin prayers, mumbling to himself, refusing to have the prayers of any but the Roman Catholicks, went up the ladder, and with the help of the hangman, made an end to his wicked days in this world. After him Winter went up the scaffold, and staid not long for his execution. Then came Graunt, who followed him, showing how so bloody a religion can make such bloody consciences. Then came Bates, and when he was hanged the Executioners prepared to Draw and Quarter them; and when this was done the business of the day was ended.

St Paul's Churchyard was the scene of the execution of Father Garnet, another Gunpowder Plot conspirator – there was some doubt that Garnet had been part of the plot, or if he was, he had been certain that it would not be carried out. On the 3 May 1606 Garnet was placed on a hurdle and brought here. Garnet who had spent nearly three months in the Tower, said a courteous goodbye to those who had served him. The hurdle was drawn by three horses from the Tower while Garnet lay on it with his hands held together and his eyes closed in prayer through streets lined with onlookers.

St Paul's Churchyard. It was at the western end of the churchyard (far end of the church in the photo) that four of the Gunpowder Plot participants were executed.

The execution took place at the western end of the churchyard opposite the Bishop's Palace. Attending Garnet, concerned that he would express regret that an attempt had been made on the king and his authority, were the Recorder of London, the Dean of St Paul's, and the Dean of Winchester. They had been instructed by the king to attend 'to assist Garnet with such advice as suited the condition of a dying man'. The scaffold was built higher than usual so that the assembled crowd could enjoy the spectacle, and hear the condemned man express his regret. There are differing accounts as to how Garnet met his death. Those sympathetic to Garnet portray him as a quiet, resigned martyr bravely meeting his fate. The account in *State Trials and Proceedings*, though biased in the report of the execution, has more than a ring of truth about it. He mounted the scaffold looking 'much amazed, fear and guiltiness appearing in his face'.

> The Dean of Paul's and Winchester being present, very gravely and Christianly exhorted him to a true and lively faith to God-ward, a free and plain acknowledgement to the world of his offence, and if any further treason lay in his knowledge, to unburden his conscience, and show a sorrow and detestation of it: but Garnet impatient of persuasions, and ill-pleased to be exhorted by them, desired them not to trouble him, he came prepared and was resolved.

Garnet was then led to the corner of the scaffold by the Recorder of London to make his confession and apologies to the surrounding crowd. The deans suggested that he should declare his repentance to the crowd, but Garnet informed them that he felt weak and unable to speak to the people as his voice failed him. The Recorder responded,

> 'Mr. Garnet, if you will come with me, I will take care that they shall hear you,' and, going before him, led him to the western end of the scaffold. He still hesitated to address the people, but the Recorder urged him to speak his mind freely, promising to repeat his words aloud to the multitude. Garnet then addressed the crowd as follows:
> 'My good fellow-citizens – I am come hither, on the morrow of the invention of the Holy Cross, to see an end of all my pains and troubles in this world. I here declare before you all that I consider the late treason and conspiracy against the State to be cruel and detestable; and, for my part, all designs and endeavours against the king were ever misliked by me; and if this attempt had been perfected, as it was designed, I think it would have been altogether damnable; and I pray for all prosperity to the king, the queen, and the royal family.'
> Here he paused, and the Recorder reminded him to ask pardon of the King for that which he had attempted. 'I do so,' said Garnet, 'as far as I have sinned against him – namely, in that I did not reveal that whereof I had a general knowledge from Mr. Catesby, but not otherwise.' Then said the Dean of Winchester, 'Mr. Garnet, I pray you deal clearly in the matter: you were certainly privy to the whole business.' 'God forbid !' said Garnet; 'I never understood anything of the design of blowing up the Parliament House.'

A key fact at his trial was that he heard the confession of the proposed plot from one of the conspirators, did not reveal it to the authorities, and was therefore privy to the plan. Garnet claimed that what he heard in confession was private, and not to be repeated. This matter came up on the scaffold:

> 'Nay,' responded the Dean of Winchester, 'it is manifest that all the particulars were known to you, and you have declared under your own hand that Greenaway told you all the circumstances in Essex.' 'That,' said Garnet, 'was in secret confession, which I could by no means reveal.' Then said the Dean, 'You have yourself, Mr. Garnet, almost acknowledged that this was only a pretence, for you have openly confessed that Greenaway told you not in a confession, but by way of a confession, and that he came of purpose to you with the design of making a confession; but you answered that it was not necessary you should know the full extent of his knowledge.'

It is likely that Garnet was slowing events in the belief that he would be reprieved. There had been rumours in London that the execution would not take place:

> Then addressing himself to execution he kneeled to pray. When he stood up, the Recorder finding in his behaviour as it were an expectation of pardon, wished him not to deceive himself, nor beguile his own soul, he was come to die, and he must die. He required him not to equivocate with his last breath; if he knew anything that might be a danger to the King or State, he should now utter it. Garnet replied that he did not now equivocate, and more than he had confessed he did not know.

Garnet then ascended the ladder and prayed. It was while he prayed that the ladder was pulled away. He was fortunate in that a number of those present rushed forward to pull on his legs to ensure he was dead before being quartered.

11. Smithfield

Smithfield is situated within walking distance of the former Newgate Gaol, and was once a primary place of execution. Stow, writing in 1598, says of Smithfield that '... in a place then called the Elms ... this had been the place of execution for offenders ... Since which time the building there hath been so increased that now remaineth not one tree growing'. Stow then describes an area given over to fairs, celebrations and jousting. One of the first recorded is that of a William FitzOsbert, otherwise known as 'Longbeard', who was hanged at the Elms in Cow Lane in 1196. It was at Smithfield that the final act of the Peasants' Revolt of 1381 took place when its leader, Wat Tyler, met the fourteen-year-old King Richard II for 'negotiations'. Contemporary reports of the events are unreliable and vary, but the general tenor is that Tyler approached the king on horseback in an 'insolent manner', throwing his dagger in the air, and attempted to grab hold of the reins of the king's horse. Sir William Walworth, the Mayor of London, alarmed that the king would be harmed, ran his sword through Tyler's neck, while another attendant of the king leapt at Tyler, stabbing him in the side. Tyler was taken by some of the rebels into the church of St Bartholomew the Great or into St Bartholomew's Hospital, but he was almost immediately dragged out again and beheaded.

Jack Straw, Tyler's second in command, was hanged in Smithfield. After the gallows were moved, Smithfield still remained as a place associated with death, particularly in the sixteenth century during the reigns of Henry VIII and Mary I. Many of the burnings for heresy took place here during Mary's short reign, 1553–58. A dramatic and comprehensive description of the lives and deaths of a presumed 278 Protestant deaths at this time can be found in the *Book of Martyrs*, written by John Foxe and published in 1563; it is violently anti-Roman Catholic. There have been numerous subsequent editions, which deal with many of the executions which took place at Smithfield

One particularly unusual execution which took place here was that of Richard Rose, a cook at the Bishop of Rochester's palace. It was alleged that Rose had poisoned 'a diverse number of persons to the number of sixteen or more ... among the which Benet Curwine, gentleman, was one, and he intended to poison the bishop himself, but he ate no pottage that day, whereby he escaped; but of the poor people that ate thereof many died'. Richard Rose, as a prisoner, was boiled alive.

Memorial to the martyrs in Smithfield.

Wat Tyler's death. Left to right: Sir William Walworth, Mayor of London (wielding sword); Wat Tyler; King Richard II; and Sir John Cavendish, Esquire to the King.

Memorial to the execution of William Wallace, who was probably executed at Tyburn, not Smithfield.

12. Wapping

Execution Dock at Wapping was on the Thames around a mile to the west of the Tower of London. Finding Wapping Old and New Stairs needs a methodical approach–that of walking down the high street on the Thames side until one finds the gaps between the buildings. Some care is needed as Wapping Old Stairs is still open to the Thames, and can be wet and slippery. The solitude of the place is rewarding and it is not difficult, with the aid of seventeenth- and eighteenth-century engravings, to picture the crowds, the smells, and the noise of those days. Wapping tube station is in the immediate vicinity as are the two famous pubs, the Prospect of Whitby and the Captain Kidd, vying in their claims to be on the site of the gallows.

Of Wapping, in 1598 Stow tells us in his *Survey of London*,

> From this precinct of St.Katherine to Wapping in the Wose (Wash) the usual place of execution for hanging of pirates and sea rovers, at the low water mark, and there to remain till three tides have overflowed them was never a house standing within these forty years; but since the gallows being after removed farther off, a continual street or filthy strait passage with alleys of small tenements, or cottages built, inhabited by sailors victuallers along by the river of Thames a good mile from the Tower.

Wapping High Street and the Captain Kidd public house. A little further along on the left are Wapping Old Stairs, which lead down to the foreshore, in the vicinity of which stood the gallows for hanging pirates.

Captain Kidd pub and foreshore. The gallows were probably located at the further end of the picture where the foreshore is deeper, nearer to Wapping Old Stairs.

Executions at Wapping

Executions at Wapping were just as laden with ritual than as those of Newgate and Tyburn processions. A magazine article of 1844 describes the procedure:

> Execution Dock, at Wapping, was devoted to the punishment of such criminals as had been guilty of capital offences on the 'high seas'. It was not uncommon, and from its frequency, scarcely considered a shocking, occurrence in the streets of London, to meet a wagon, or rather, what is called a 'Thames-street cart', moving at a slow pace along the street, and conveying some unhappy culprit to the place of execution. The cart contained also the offender's coffin placed before his eyes, and the chaplain, praying aloud, and exhorting him to repentance. The mournful procession, in which a silver oar, and other symbols of authority, were exhibited, surrounded by a crowd of idlers, arrived at Execution Dock, and in a few minutes the convict was seen struggling between life and death. The tide beneath the criminal was nearly at its lowest ebb, when the executioner cast him off, and the body had to remain until the river touched his feet: sometimes it was allowed to reach his knees. It was then cut down, and placed in the same cart, with a piece of black cloth flung carelessly across it, paraded through the city, and deposited in Hicks' Hall. For the next week the body of the unhappy convict lay for the inspection of the curious and sight-seeing public, cut and mangled, dissected and anatomised – a sickening spectacle to the multitude who crowded to see it, and linger in the gallery to cast down one more look upon the revolting scene …When every seeker of medical knowledge, from the experienced surgeon to the thoughtless student, had dabbled in the blood of the criminal, the body, mangled and hideous as it was to view, was loaded with chains, and suspended from one of the gibbets which lined the banks of the river in the olden time. 'That is my old messmate, Tom Brown,' or, 'There hangs my fellow-apprentice, Jack Smith,' the sailors would say, as they passed down the

Thames. Every corpse, disfigured and mutilated though it was, was well known; and as the watermen rowed their boats along the river, they would occasionally pull a little out of their way, to drive off the birds that were greedily devouring the body of some old companion.

An entry in Henry Machyn's diary of the '6th day of April [1557] was hanged at the low-water marke at Wapping beyond saint Katherines 7 [persons] for robbing on the sea'.

In *Mist's Weekly Journal* on 14 May 1726,

Yesterday Captain Jeane was hang'd at Execution-Dock, for the barbarous murther of his cabbin-boy, and was afterwards hang'd in chains on the river-side, over against Cuckold's Point. When the time of his suffering this deserved death drew nigh, he often fell into such violent fits in Newgate that 'twas thought he would have died there.

One of the most famous executions to take place at Wapping was that of Captain William Kidd (*c.* 1645–23 May 1701) for murder and five counts of piracy. Kidd at his Old Bailey trial protested his innocence and petitioned the reigning monarchs, William and Mary, to no avail. Papers that would have saved him at his trial had been misfiled, and actually did come to light in the twentieth century. Kidd and a number of colleagues were sentenced to be hanged at Execution Dock. The execution took place

An engraving from the *Newgate Calendar,* or *'Malefactor's Register'*, depicting a pirate execution at Wapping.

View from the Captain Kidd pub today.

on the Tuesday 23 May 1701. Eight of his colleagues received reprieves, but Kidd and one of his crewmen, Darby Mullins had their sentences confirmed. They were taken in a pair of horse-drawn carts led by the Admiralty marshal carrying the silver oar through a large London crowd. As the *Newgate Calendar* observes, 'a circumstance happened at his execution that will be worthy of recital':

> After he had been tied up to the gallows, the rope broke, and he fell to the ground; but being immediately tied up again, the ordinary, who had before exhorted him, desired to speak with him once more; and on this second application, entreated him to make the most careful use of the few farther moments thus providentially allotted him for the final preparation of his soul to meet its important change. These exhortations appeared to have the wished-for effect; and he was left, professing his charity to all the world, and his hopes of salvation through the merits of his redeemer.

Location of the Gallows

The comment by Stow that the gallows had been removed 'farther off' indicates that the gallows had no fixed point, and were set up in the area between the modern-day Captain Kidd public house and the Prospect of Whitby public house, a little further to the east along Wapping High Street. *Old London* observes that,

> Pirates were hung at East Wapping as early as the reign of Henry VI., for in a *Chronicle of London*, edited by Sir Harris Nicolas, we read that in this reign two bargemen were hung beyond St. Katherine's, for murdering three Flemings and a child in a Flemish vessel; 'and there they hengen till the water had washed them by ebbying and flowyd, so the water bett upon them.' And as late as 1735 we read in

the Gentleman's Magazine, 'Williams the pirate was hanged at Execution Dock, and afterwards in chains at Bugsby's Hole, near Blackwall.' Howell, in his *Londinopolis*, 1657, says, 'From the Liberties of St. Katherine to Wapping, 'tis yet in the memory of man, there never was a house standing but the gallowes, which was further removed in regard of the buildings. But now there is a continued street, towards a mile long, from the Tower all along the river, almost as far as Radcliffe, which proceedeth from the increase of navigation, mariners, and trafique.'

Rocque's 1746 map of London gives Execution Dock as approximately 200 yards east of Wapping New Stairs. It is possible that this was an access point from the New Stairs. Contemporary accounts speak of the bodies of dead pirates hanging on gibbets that lined the entrance to east London on the river itself. The Rocque map shows two pairs of these gibbets.

13. Kennington Common

Kennington is situated approximately 2 miles south of Westminster via Westminster Bridge. The former place of execution is situated directly opposite the Oval Tube Station on a site now occupied by St Mark's Church. Between 1678 and 1799 129 executions are recorded there.

The brooding presence of St Mark's Church opposite the Oval Tube Station marks the site of the gallows where at least 129 people were executed between 1678 and 1799.

Gibbet on Kennington Common, around 1748.

The first execution we know about was that of Sarah Elston who was burned in 1678 for having murdered her husband. The last was that of a fraudster named Badger who was hanged in 1799. The church was built on the site with the work commencing in 1822, and being completed in 1824.

The Common is described in the *Tour Round London*, in 1774 as

> a small spot of ground on the road to Camberwell, and about a mile and a half from London. Upon this spot is erected the gallows for the county of Surrey; but few have suffered here of late years. Such of the (Scottish) rebels as were tried by the Special Commission, in 1746, and ordered for execution, suffered at this place; amongst whom were those who commanded the regiment raised at Manchester for the use (service) of the Pretender. In fact, very many of those who had 'been out' in the Scottish rising of the previous year here suffered the last penalty of the law. Among them were Sir John Wedderburn, John Hamilton, Andrew Wood, and Alexander Leith, and also two English gentlemen of good family, named Towneley and Fletcher, who had joined the standard of 'Bonny Prince Charlie' at Manchester. (fn. 5) Wood, it is said, bravely drank a glass to the 'Pretender's' health on the scaffold. Others engaged in the same cause also suffered here; among them Captain James (or, as he is still called, 'Jemmy') Dawson, over whose body, as soon as the headsman's axe had done its terrible work, a young lady, who was attached to him tenderly, threw herself in a swoon, and died literally of a broken heart.

Old and New London provides further information, giving a graphic account of the manner in which the Scottish rebels were dealt with on Kennington Common:

Dawson and eight others were dragged on hurdles from the new gaol in Southwark to Kennington Common, and there hanged. After being suspended for three minutes from the gallows, their bodies were stripped naked and cut down, in order to undergo the operation of beheading and disembowelling. Colonel Towneley was the first that was laid upon the block, but the executioner observing the body to retain some signs of life, he struck it violently on the breast, for the humane purpose of rendering it quite insensible for the remaining portion of the punishment. This not having the desired effect, he cut the unfortunate gentleman's throat. The shocking ceremony of heart and throwing the bowels into the fire was then gone through, after which the head was separated from the body with a cleaver, and both were put into a coffin. The rest of the bodies were thus treated in succession; and on throwing the last heart into the fire, which was that of young Dawson, the executioner cried, "God save King George!" and the spectators responded with a shout. Although the rabble had hooted the unhappy gentlemen on the passage to and from their trials, it was remarked that at the execution their fate excited considerable pity, mingled with admiration of their courage. Two circumstances contributed to increase the public sympathy on this occasion, and caused it to be more generally expressed. The first was, the appearance at the place of execution of a youthful brother of one of the culprits, of the name of Deacon, himself a culprit, and under sentence of death for the same crime, but who had been permitted to attend the last scene of his brother's life in a coach along with a guard. The other was the fact of a young and beautiful woman, to whom Dawson had been betrothed, actually attending to witness his execution, as stated above.

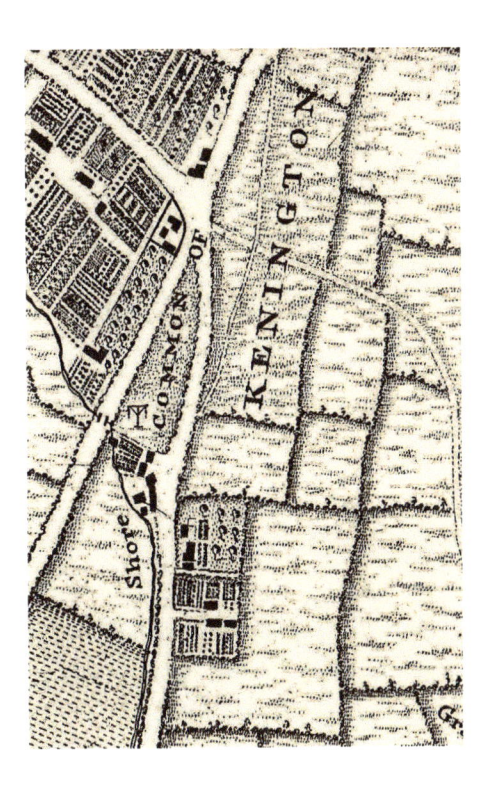

Rocque 1746 map showing the gibbet on the Common.

A *'Survey of London,'* 1956, tells us that the area around St Mark's Church was where the gallows once stood. 'The common land in Kennington lay on the south-eastern border of the Manor, and is now covered by St Mark's Church and burial ground, the triangle of land between Brixton and Kennington Park Roads, and a large part of Kennington Park.' In the eighteenth and nineteenth centuries Kennington Common gained an evil reputation. Part of it, including the site of the church and burial ground and the triangle of land between Brixton and Kennington Park Roads, was used as a place of execution and known as Gallows Common. Several Jacobites were executed here after the rising of 1745, and in 1866 when the removal of Temple Bar from Fleet Street was being considered, there was a suggestion that it should be re-erected in the Park to commemorate their execution.

The Site Today

St Mark's Church and the very pleasant Kennington Park that lies adjacent to the church are easily accessible by tube and car. The church is opposite the Oval Tube Station, and is a ten-minute journey by car south from Westminster. Of the gallows there are no reminders.

14. Some Other London Places of Execution

Horsemonger Lane Prison served what was the county of Surrey. It was constructed between 1791 and 1799 and had the novel method of staging its executions on the flat roof of the prison's gatehouse. The prison contained only one cell for the condemned. The jail was demolished in 1878, but between 1800 and 1877, accounted for the execution of 131 men and 4 women. The site of the jail is a park, Newington Gardens, in the vicinity of the Inner London Crown Court.

The early records tantalisingly refer to places of execution which rarely appear on the early maps. A reference by Henry Machyn in his diary entry of 12 April 1554 concerning the fate of Thomas Wyatt's head tells us that his head was 'set upon the gallows on *Hay-hyll* beside Hyde Park; where did hang three men in chains upon a stake'. Foxe's *Book of Martyrs* tells us that in the immediate aftermath of the Wyatt rebellion, gallows were set up in Cheapside, and that on the 13 February 1554, 'were set up a great number of gallowses in divers places of the city; namely, two in Cheapside, one at Leadenhall, one at Billingsgate, one at St.Magnus Church, one in Smithfield, one in Fleet Street, four in Southwark, one at Aldgate, one at Bishopsgate, one at St James's Park corner, one at Cripplegate: and which gibbets and gallowses, to the number of twenty, there remained for terror of others from the thirteenth of February till the fourth of June and then, at the coming in of King Philip [of Spain], were taken down'.

Indeed, gallows could, and sometimes would, appear anywhere in London. Some examples from an 1856 history of London, and the punishment of its criminals, tells us that the gallows could be set up 'before your own door in every part of the town'. It mentions, among many others, gallows being set up on 14 September 1741 for the execution of James Hall at the end of Catherine Street in the Strand, of an execution at the foot of Bow Street in 1760, another at Chiswell Street, Finsbury, in 1767 and an execution opposite the end of Panton Street in the Haymarket.

More Gallows

Old and New London, 1878, tells us with regards to the location of some of London's places of execution,

> ...sixty years before the death of Cromwell [1658] the gallows were frequently erected at the extremity of St Giles's parish, near the end of the present Tottenham Court Road; while for nearly two centuries the Holborn end of Fetter Lane, within a short distance of Red Lion Square, was no less frequently the place of execution. Indeed, in 1643, only a few years before the exhumation and gibbeting of Cromwell, we find Nathaniel Tomkins executed at this spot for his share in Waller's plot to surprise the City. In addition, however, to these surmises is the curious fact of the bodies of Cromwell and Ireton having been brought in carts, on the night previous to their exposure on the gibbet, to the Red Lion Inn, Holborn, from which Red Lion Square derives its name, where they rested during the night. In taking this step, it is surely not unreasonable to presume that the Government had in view the selection of a house in the immediate vicinity of the scaffold, in order that the bodies might be in readiness for the disgusting exhibition of the following morning. Supposing this to have been the case, the place of their exposure and interment could scarcely have been the end of Tyburn Lane, inasmuch as the distance thither from Westminster is actually shorter than the distance from Westminster to Red Lion Square. The object of the Government could hardly have been to create a sensation by parading the bodies along a populous thoroughfare, inasmuch as the ground between St Giles's Pound and Tyburn, a distance of a mile and a half, was at this period almost entirely open country.

The 1856 *Gentleman's Magazine* article tells us that 'at an early date, even when St Giles's was the regular place [of execution] ... there were gallows and occasional executions at Shepherd's Bush, when Tybourn succeeded St Giles'.

> Thursday, April 30. Yesterday Drumond and Shrimpton, lately hanged in chains on Stamford-hill, were removed with their gibbet to a remote part of the Common, near the place where Joseph Still was hanged in the like manner. [*Grub-street Journal*, 7 May 1730]

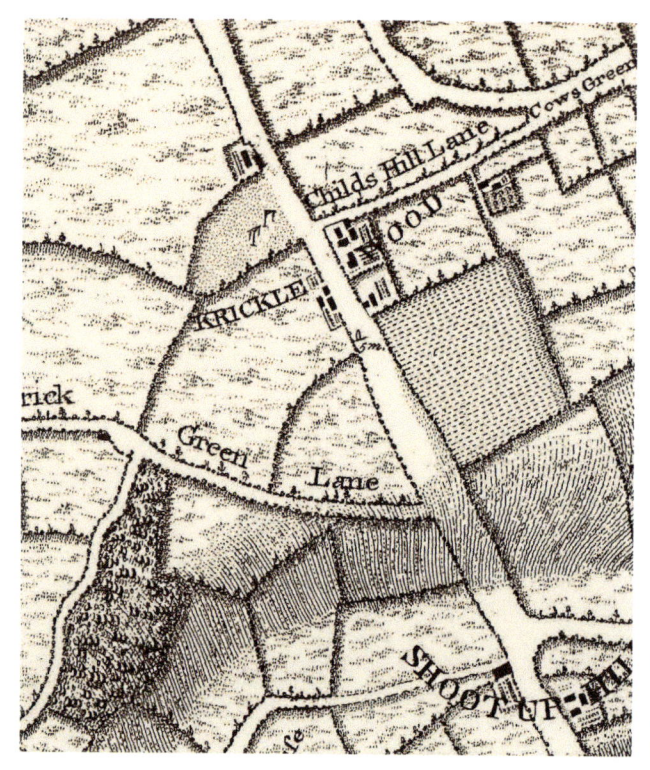

Rocque's map of 1746 depicts a double gibbet and a gallows on the corner of Cricklewood Broadway and Chichele Road.

Rocque's map of 1746 shows gallows and gibbet at the eastern end of Shepherd's Bush Green.

The *Newgate Calendar* refers to the execution of 'JAMES WHITNEY Notorious Highwayman, who believed in dressing well' at 'Porters Block' near Smithfield. Porter's Block was in St John's Street.

A nineteenth-century history of London makes reference to an execution on the corner of Long Lane and Barbican. A memorial stone could be seen affixed to the cornerstone of a linen-draper's house at the site which read,

> On Saturday, 20 Nov.1790, the two incendiaries were executed, who wilfully set on fire, on the sixteenth May in the same year, several houses which stood on this ground, and occasioned a loss of upwards of £40,000, for no other purpose but to plunder the sufferes.

And,

> A Person named Flindall, then detected in stealing, wrote a letter to Mr. Alderman Skinner, which led to the disclosure of the whole particulars of that calamity. Flindall being admitted king's evidence, it also appears that this act of villainy had no other object than that of plunder. Edward Love and William Jobbins, being convicted of this crime at the Old Bailey on the 30th October, was executed on the spot where the depredation was committed, on the 20 November 1790, and confessed their guilt at the place of execution.

There were gallows situated on the corner of the Edgware Road (Cricklewood Broadway) and Chichele Road, NW2, where Oaklands Road meets The Broadway. There were gallows situated at the western end of Shepherd's Bush Green near to the Holland Park roundabout. On Hampstead Heath the gibbet was strung between two elm trees quite near to Jack Straw's Castle, formerly a public house, on the left of the road to North End.

Bibliography

(1717). *The History of the Press-Yard, or, a brief account of the customs and occurrences that are put in practice ... in that ancient repository of living bodies called ... Newgate*, etc, London.

Andrews, A., *The Eighteenth Century; or, Illustrations of the manners and customs of our grandfathers* (London: Chapman & Hall, 1856) pp. x. 334.

Canning, G. and W. R. L. Russell, (1763). An epistle from William Lord Russell to William Lord Cavendish; written in Newgate, on Friday night, July twentieth, 1683. London, printed for the author; and sold by R. and J. Dodsley, T. Becket and P. A. de Hondt, and C. Henderson.

Challoner, R. B. o. D., T. G. Law, et al. (1742). *Memoirs of Missionary Priests, and of other Catholics, that have suffered death in England, on religious accounts, from ... 1577 to 1684.* [By R. Challoner, Bishop of Debra.], 2 pt. [London,] 1741.

Chambers, R. *The book of days: a miscellany of popular antiquities in connection with the calendar including anecdote, biography, and history curiosities of literature and oddities of human life and character*, [S. l.],: W. & R. Chambers, (1869).

Clayton, J. W. and K. o. E. A. B. I. G. Charles Ii (1859). *Personal Memoirs of Charles the Second; with sketches of his court and times.* [With portraits.], 2 vol. C. J. Skeet: London.

Cobbett, W. M. P., T. B. Howell, et al. (1809). Cobbett's Complete Collection of *State Trials and Proceedings* for High Treason High Treason and other Crimes and Misdemeanors from the earliest period to the present time, (vol. 11-21. A Complete Collection of State Trials ... with notes and other illustrations compiled by T. B. Howell.-vol. 22-33. A Complete Collection of State Trials ... from the earliest period to the year 1783 with notes and other illustrations: compiled by T. B. Howell ... and continued from the year 1783 to the present time: by Thomas Jones Howell.), 33 vol. R. Bagshaw: Longman & Co.: London.

Freeman, E. A. and M. Paris (1883). *Chronicles and memorials of Great Britain, Matthaei Parisiensis ... edited by Henry Richards Luard.*

Gatrell, V. A. C. (1994). *The hanging tree: execution and the English people, 1770-1868*. Oxford, Oxford University Press.

Grey, J. L., J. G. Nichols, et al. (1850). *The Chronicle of Queen Jane, and of two years of Queen Mary, and especially of the rebellion of Sir Thomas Wyat*. Written by a Resident in the Tower of London. Edited by J. G. Nichols, London.

Holinshed, R. (1577). The firste volume of the chronicles of England, Scotlande, and Irelande, conteyning the description and chronicles of England, from the first inhabiting unto the Conquest. B. L, London: Imprinted for John Harrison.

Hooper, W. E. (1935). *History of Newgate and the Old Bailey*, etc. [S.l.], [s.n.].

John Foxe, J. C. (1559, 1844 ed.). Fox's Book of Martyrs: The Acts and Monuments of the Church G. Virtue.

Johnson, C. C. p. (1734). A General History of the Lives and Adventures of the Most Famous Highwaymen, Murderers, Street-Robbers, &c. London: J. Janeway.

Knight, C. P. (1864). *Passages of a Working Life during half a century; with a prelude of early reminiscences*, 3 vol. London.

Machyn, H. and J. G. Nichols (1848). *The Diary of H. Machyn, Citizen and Merchant Taylor of London, from A.D. 1550 to A.D. 1563*. Edited by J.G. Nichols, London.

Marks, A. (1908). *Tyburn Tree: its history and annals*. [With illustrations.], pp. xi. 292. Brown, Langham & Co.: London.

Nichols, J. G., T. A. o. C. A. Cranmer, et al. (1859). Narratives of the days of the Reformation, chiefly from the manuscripts of John Foxe the Martyrologist; with two contemporary biographies of Archbishop Cranmer. Edited by J. G. Nichols, London.

Nichols, J. G. and Franciscans (1852). *Chronicle of the Grey Friars of London*, London.

Nottingham, H. F. E. o. (1660). An exact and most impartial accompt of the indictment, arraignment, trial, and judgment (according to law) of nine and twenty regicides the murtherers of His late sacred Majesty of most glorious memory. London, Printed for Andrew Crook and Edward Powel.

Pelham, C. (1891). *The Chronicles of crime*. [S. l.], Miles.

Platter, T. (1937). *Thomas Platter's Travels in England 1599*, London, Jonathan Cape.

Roberts, G. o. L. R. (1844). *The Life, Progresses, and Rebellion of James, Duke of Monmouth, to his capture and execution: with a full account of the Bloody Assize, and copious biographical notices*, 2 vol. London.

Stanhope, P. H. t. E. S. (1836). *History of England from the Peace of Utrecht (to the Peace of Versailles)*, etc, 7 vol. London.

Stow, J. (2005). *A survey of London: written in the year 1598*. Stroud, Sutton Publishing.

Stow, J. H. a. A. and W. J. Thoms (1842). [*A survey of the cities of London and Westminster ... brought down from the year 1633 ... to the present time by J. Strype. To which is prefixed the life of the author by the editor, etc.*], London.

Thompson, E. M. S. G. C. B. D. a. P. L. o. t. B. M. (1889). *Adæ Murimuth Continuatio Chronicarum. Robertus de Avesbury De Gestis mirabilibus Regis Edwardi Tertii.* Edited by Edward Maunde Thompson, pp. lxiii. 515. London.

Tytler, P. F. (1833). *Life of Sir Walter Raleigh*. Edinburgh, Oliver and Boyd Tweeddale Court.

Tytler, P. F. (1837). *Life of King Henry the Eighth*. Edinburgh, Oliver & Boyd.

Walford, E. (1984). *Village London: the story of Greater London*. Vol.1. London, Alderman Press.